Wisdom, Bliss
and
Common Sense

Cover photo by Floyd Kettering

Wisdom, Bliss
and
Common Sense

Secrets of Self-Transformation

*This publication is made possible with
the assistance of the Kern Foundation*

**The Theosophical Publishing House
Wheaton, Ill. U.S.A.
Madras, India/London, England**

The Theosophical Publishing House
306 West Geneva Road
Wheaton, IL 60187

A publication of the Theosophical Publishing House, a
department of the Theosophical Society in America.

Library of Congress Cataloging in Publication Data

Deane, Darshani.
    Wisdom, bliss, and common sense : secrets of self-
transformation /
    Darshani Deane. -- 1st ed.
        p.   cm.
    "A Quest original;--T.p. verso.
    ISBN 0-8356-0644-9 : $8.50
    1. Spiritual life. I. Title.
BL624.D386   1989   88-40485
291.4'48--dc19   CIP

Printed in the United States of America

Contents

3. Principles of Truth

Prologue

The other day somebody asked me how long it took me to write this book. I gave him three answers: forty days, for one; in a truer sense, ten years; in a still truer sense, a quarter of a century.

During the past decade I have given workshops for the public and for industry, churches, hospitals, and schools on personal growth and the dynamics of spirituality. Some of my self-transformation sessions are on anger and the spiritual way. Others deal with anxiety, fear, guilt, suffering, relationships—and the spiritual way. All kinds of people come: corporate executives; counselors; college students; teachers; housewives; office cleaners; insurance, real estate and car salespeople; lay persons; clergy; atheists; and the poor, rich, unschooled, and erudite. Yet no matter who they are or what they do, they ask the same questions and fight the same inner battles. Over and over again, I have heard people say:

"I have no self-discipline."

"Why should they treat me like this? I don't deserve it!"

"I have a right to be angry. Look at what he did to me!"

"If only things were different! If only I didn't have this problem!"

"Death? I can't deal with it."

"I feel so guilty—I wish I hadn't done it."

"I'm jealous, and I can't help it."

"How can I stop judging when I know that the guy is a bad egg?"

After leading workshops for ten years, the thought occurred to me that if the same problems plague people I met, surely they must plague people whom I had not met. That sparked the realization that if I published the questions that kept coming up, along with my replies, I might help more people than I could ever meet in person. Through memory, notes, and recordings, I began. That draft was the dawn of *Wisdom, Bliss, and Common Sense*, Part 1—"Getting Out of Your Own Way."

When I finished writing Part 1, I considered the workshops I give on spiritual dynamics. Seekers from all traditions come to these sessions: church-going Christians who want spiritual experience; seekers on the Vedic, Buddhist, Taoist, Kabbalist, mystical Christian, Gurdjieff, and pathless paths; and would-be meditators who want to know what, why, when, where, and how. Their questions repeat themselves just as much as those in the transformation workshops do:

"How can I let go and let God? Look at my responsibilities!"

"I've been meditating for so long, and nothing happens."

"Do we or don't we have free will?"

"I've been to a lot of workshops, but I still don't know what meditation is all about."

"I do fine on the meditation seat, but when I get to the office, the peace vanishes."

"I've tried so many paths that I'm confused."

"How can you love your enemy in today's world?"

"What does liberation really mean?"

These and similar questions, along with my answers, became Part 2—"The Dynamics of Spiritual Growth," and Part 3—"Principles of Truth."

My replies are based on approaches to enlightenment and self-transformation practiced for centuries in Vedic, Buddhist, and Christian monasteries. They bear little or no resemblance to contemporary modes of transformation such as conventional therapy, which tends to confine itself to "mind reforming mind." Mind, with its mechanical movements, cannot reform itself. Mind needs to open, to cultivate a hospitality to a force field that functions on a plane above itself. *That* reforms.

The ancestry of my replies dates back twenty-five years to my first year in India. Nestled in the foothills of the Himalayas along the banks of the Ganges is the Sivananda Ashram where for several hours every day I listened to the wisdom of His Holiness, Sri Swami Krishnanandaji. I had not planned any of this. In fact, I was trying to be the first woman to drive alone around the world. London was my starting point. I had painted "Eastward Ho!" on a door of my Land Rover and worked my way as a professional accordionist from country to country throughout Europe and the Middle East. I reached India two and a half years later. Two months after that—and only because I thought it would make a good chapter in my travel book—I drove up the long winding driveway of the Sivananda Ashram.

Swami Krishnanandaji was giving a daily discourse on *The Panchadasi*, a standard text on Vedanta. Of course, I had never heard of Vedanta. But then I had no idea of what an ashram was, or even a swami. As he spoke about the nondual existence of *Brahman*, the infinite, self-luminous Consciousness, the Knower— the only Reality there is—I felt as though I had lived all my life in a room with the shades drawn over the windows and suddenly the shades were going up.

Light streamed in and it woke me up. I was thirty-five years old.

Brahman was so exciting to me. To experience and know it as my Self, to know that I am limitless Being and Consciousness, not a limited body subject to birth and death—here was something to live for. Here was the value in life and of life. The beauty of Brahman was that this great value did not exist outside of me. It depended neither on somebody else's whims, loves, or moods, nor on any external or internal condition. It was my Self, "I" was Brahman. "I" am Brahman. "I" will always be Brahman. That changeless Reality was what I had been seeking when I worked my way through Europe and through Africa from the southern tip of Cape Town to Cairo in the north—*just in case, God forbid, I might miss something*—looking, searching everywhere, and never finding.

Of course, the quest went back long before that to Queens, New York, where I was born. It went back to my third birthday when my folks gave me a jack-in-the-box toy, and I screamed and sobbed, "That's me! I'm in the box, and I want to get out!" On my eighth birthday they discovered that I was "a born musician" and bought me an accordion that would one day open the lid on jack-in-the-box. While the kids outside jumped rope, I practiced scales. My teacher insisted that I play like a one-woman orchestra. There would be no oompah-pahs or polkas for me. I was taught to play classics and good jazz and to compose. Through music I could express a truth inside of me—a yearning, a reaching out for something I could not articulate.

Like most people in the world, I began to think that joy could be found in success and in all the dramas that fill other peoples' lives. There were television, radio, and night club performances in New York, Chicago, and Palm Beach; university years in the arts and premedicine; men, marriage, an addiction to chess, and the thrill of flying a Piper Cub. But it wasn't enough. Nothing was enough. In my twenties I performed on an ocean cruiser to Scandinavia. At Oslo I jumped ship, and for three years I played television, radio, hotels, and military bases in every country on the continent. There were more men and more university years— Munich, this time—but every success and romance seemed fleeting and illusory. Only one inner pull drove me: to see the whole world and discover whether there was anything anywhere that was worth pursuing.

A contract for Johannesburg brought me to Africa. Then for two years I trekked up the continent working in Rhodesia and the Belgian Congo (as they were called then), where a safari in the Ituri forest brought me closer to my self than any place I'd seen. There was the Sudan, and Ethiopia where I played a U.S. air base, and then Djibuti in Somaliland to board a cargo liner across the Red sea into Egypt. For six months I lived in a houseboat on the Nile enjoying what I called "the free life." Then I went to Israel to spend another six months picking up turnips on a Kibbutz farm near Haifa. Here for the first time, I saw communal commitment. Commitment was precisely what I wanted. The problem was that I had nothing to be committed to.

Back in Europe I bought the Land Rover, and the long working journey eastward across Europe and the Middle East began. Almost every newspaper en route sent a reporter to interview "the lone American globetrotter who mixed jazz and auto mechanics" (all I knew how to do was to clean out the air filter and change my tires). But no thrill, no adventure, no delight or joy lasted. A "low" followed every "high" until the day I drove up that Himalayan driveway in India and heard the word "Brahman."

After that my appetite for knowledge was insatiable. I received initiation and learned how to concentrate and meditate. Under the guidance of Swami Krishnanandaji, I studied Vedantic scriptures such as the *Upanishads*. I felt an intense hunger for liberation. At times I thought I would not live if I could not have the experience. My goal was clear and so was the way to reach it. But my compulsion "to leave nothing uncovered" on my inner journey nagged me as much as it had on my outer journey. I wanted to learn about other paths, how they fit into the Vedantic context, their differences and common links with one another—*just in case, God forbid, I might miss something.*

I studied different yogas and holed up in my Himalayan kutir or hut to meditate. One morning I was concentrating intensely on a crucifix. Suddenly it vanished from my consciousness, and I felt an ecstasy and sweetness that made worldly joys seem like toys. "If this keeps up," I told my teacher, "I'll be realized in six months." He picked up a book, stuck a marker in a page, and said, "Go to your kutir and read this." When I looked at the title I was crushed: "Humility is the hallmark of progress."

Renunciation was the key, I thought. I burned my theatrical gowns, Western clothes, and makeup, donned Indian robes, and told my teacher I was staying forever. "I'm through with the world," I said. In a voice that shook my self-assurance, he asked, "What makes you think that the world is through with you?" I walked back to my room wondering why that mattered. Surely all that counted was that *I* was through with the world.

Cobras, rats, scorpions, visa hassles (I had gone all the way to the late Prime Minister Nehru for the last extension), and dwindling funds were chronic problems. But all I could think of was God-Realization. I figured if I could attain enlightenment before my money ran out, I'd have it made. One day a palmist looked at my hand. ''You travel a lot,'' he said. ''I did or I will?'' I asked. ''Both,'' he said. Sure enough, a year later I was heading north to Nepal. In Kathmandu a Jesuit priest told me of a job at a Tibetan refugee camp. ''Doing what?'' I asked. ''Everything,'' he said. I had one fifty-dollar bill left. ''I'll take it.''

At the camp I fixed up a meditation hut, but I seldom got there. I started and ran a school and a clinic, gave daily injections of vitamin B for beri-beri, raised funds, and drove in and out of Kathmandu for supplies. That was a treacherous stretch. Death row, I called it. Wide enough for only one vehicle, the pot-holed road was bound on one side by a wall of cascading, jagged rocks and on the other by a precipice that dropped down thousands of feet to where you could see crushed trucks and cars. I prayed fiercely. I chanted my mantra loudly. I was scared I might die before I'd realized. I wasn't ready. To be ready, you had to have God in your mind and on your lips all the time so it would be there at the crucial moment of death. How could I do that? My mind was filled with the camp.

In Kathmandu I would see Jesuit Father Moran and Reverend Lama Serkong Rimpochen who taught me about Tibetan Buddhism. ''Life gets in the way,'' I told them. ''Be like us,'' Father would say. ''We pray five times a day. Punctuate your work with prayer.'' The Lama said I would have to incorporate strict disciplines like not eating after noon. That was impossible. ''Then don't eat after four.'' Even that I could not do. All that happened to me spiritually was the continuation of the fierce burning for realization. It was like a fire that I thought would consume me.

When the camp dissolved I sold my Land Rover and returned to India. I stayed with Ananda Moi Ma and then returned to home base at the Sivananda Ashram. "This is it," I told my teacher. "I can't make it in the world. Like Buddha under the bo-tree, I am going to sit in my kutir until I reach enlightenment. I am finished with traveling. Finished with the world!" He said again, "What makes you think the world is through with you? God and the world are not poles apart!" There, on the banks of the Ganges, surrounded by the Himalayas, spiritual experiences brought me a glimpse of Reality. More and more, the world seemed like a passing show.

A year later I found myself journeying westward. I went to the Soviet Union, to Eastern Europe, and to Italy to be in the presence of stigmata saint Padre Pio. Each time he put his hand on my head, I was overcome by a love for Jesus so intense that I wanted to cry out loud. Love tugged at my heart as if someone were pulling on it with ropes. Early mornings after Padre Pio's 4:00 A.M. Mass, I would walk the streets of that little town of San Giovanni Rotundo, yearning to enter a Carmelite monastery. But the yearning confused me. The pull to Jesus was a pull to an otherness, an inner hunger to experience and love Him in the depths of spiritual intimacy. On the other hand, my intense attraction for Brahman, the Self, the impersonal Reality that I am, pulled me another way. I felt like a person with two heads attached at the back. One head looked East; the other looked West. "I" could be in only one head at a time.

When I left Italy, I accepted an invitation from John

Bennett to stay at his institute in Coombe Springs near London to study the Gurdjieff Work and practice the movements daily. One morning, six months after I arrived, I was walking down Oxford Street in London when my consciousness suddenly rose above my head and remained poised there. My body felt like a log of wood. I was no longer in it. "I" was pure objective Consciousness, wide, unattached, uninvolved. That was the first time I truly understood what Gurdjieff meant by "objective consciousness."

I told Bennett that I wanted this on a permanent basis. "For that, I've got to go to a monastery or ashram," I said. "I can't do it in the world." He said, as he had said so many times, "Monasteries are not the way of Gurdjieff. This is the fourth way—transformation of consciousness in the world. Use the stuff of the world and your reactions as grist for your mill." But I simply could not do it. My "all or nothing at all" syndrome persisted.

After a brief visit to New York, I got on a cargo ship for a return trip to Africa, this time to a monastery. "I'm here for solitude," I told the ascetic director. "For meditation."

"You're here for work," he corrected. He handed me one hundred original letters to type. "Urgent," he said. Those were not only pre-wordprocessing days; they were pre-electric typewriter days. On an old manual I began. When I finished the letters, I could barely stay awake, but I forced myself to type the envelopes and stamp them. When I finished the last one, he appeared and picked one up. "How can we send this out? Look at them—all of them! The stamps are crooked! Soak them off, dry them, and glue them back on straight. Now. Don't ruin one envelope or one stamp."

I couldn't believe that he was serious. But he was. Five minutes later he came back. ''What is your spiritual goal?'' he asked me.

''Union with the Self,'' I said. ''Knowing I am That.'' He shook his head. ''That is not ours. Our goal here is 'perfection in action'.'' Days and months and years went on that way as he pushed me to push my body and mind to the limits of their endurance. I didn't appreciate it then. I did not know that he was dissolving the thick crust of my sense of do-ership through the act of surrender. I did not surrender to him; I surrendered the resistance of my lower nature to my higher self. His training geared me for what I would soon face.

When funds dwindled, I moved to a Black mission school in the bundu of South Africa where I taught English, raised funds, lived and meditated in a wood-and-iron shack with an outdoor toilet surrounded by five-foot high kukuyu grass. More and more I was able to bring the consciousness of God into daily life. Still, as often as I could, I went into solitude at a Christian hermitage in the Drakensberg Mountains. One day I picked up a *Who's Who* and saw that it had no Black names in it. Black friends and I decided to do a Black *Who's Who* ourselves. It meant six months, I thought. Then I would be ready to renounce—orange robes and all. Six months turned into four years. Only my endurance training and steady meditation pulled me through those challenges.

When the book was published, I took off for India the long way around. Before the ''final renunciation'' I had to see the Cameroons, Nigeria, Mexico, China, and Burma. In India this time I did not tell my teacher that I was through with the world. The lesson had gotten across. At the Sri Aurobindo Ashram in Pondicherry, the lesson of how to reconcile impersonal and personal knowledge and love, inaction and action, finally began to sink in.

Back in South Africa, an African seer said I would soon start to teach. "Me? Teach? How can I? I'm not realized yet!"

"So many people don't even know the ABC's," he said. "Do they need a Ph.D. to teach them?"

So teaching began—workshops, lectures, retreats for industry, groups, individuals. The seer was right. I was surprised that so many people did not even know that they were not their bodies and minds, that they could master their minds. One day I met the seer again. "You will go abroad soon," he said. "To teach."

I shook my head furiously. "No, no," I said. "I'm not traveling any more!"

"What you intend and what He intends are two different things," the seer said. I still hadn't learned that lesson.

To be on the safe side, I gave away my eight suitcases. A month later I had to buy one: I was off to New York with a six-week Apex ticket to address a conference on Unity and see Baba Muktananda. One evening I sat in front of a large auditorium listening to him speak. All the time I thought, "Why haven't I realized God yet? What is holding me back?" Suddenly Baba looked straight at me. "You haven't realized God because of your attachments and aversions."

"Me?" I thought. "I have no attachments and no aversions!"

"Look in your pocket," I heard him say in my mind. I pulled up a small folded calendar on which I had marked off the days to my departure. Sure enough—I could not wait to return to Africa.

"You mean," I thought, "that I am attached to a continent and a country? Is that possible?"

Baba said out loud, "You can be attached to a continent, a country, a dog, an idea. You know if you are attached by how much thought you give it, and in comparison, how much thought you give to God." He had a point. In recent years I had thought more about South Africa than about God. But at least, I said to myself, I had no aversions.

"No?" I heard Baba say in my mind. "How do you feel about staying in the United States?"

"Staying here?" I thought. I couldn't! I wouldn't! The very thought of the American rat race horrified me.

"What horrifies you," Baba said out loud, "is your aversion." His gaze pierced my eyes. I closed them and asked myself, "Do I or don't I want God-realization?" For a long time I sat silent, meditating only on that. Slowly, I opened my handbag, took out my ticket, and slipped into the line of devotees. They carried flowers and fruit to present to Baba. All I had was my ticket. When I got to the front, I handed it to him. He took it and said gently, "Are you sure you want to do this?"

Through tears, I nodded. "I want God, Baba."

I never returned to South Africa. After some months I booked myself into a Franciscan hermitage and meditated almost six hours a day. As experiences deepened, the thought came, "I'm staying in this hut forever." As soon as I surrendered to that thought, I regretted it. Within hours, the spiritual director knocked on my door and said one word, "Enough." Out on the streets with no possessions, no money, no plans, no friends, and barely able to speak after all that silence. I watched the world Sadguru take over. Suddenly I was plunged into teaching and talking—to the public, organizations, industry, retreat centers, churches, individuals. I was even composing songs about the spiritual life and peace.

Last year, after spending eight months in India, I decided that I had talked enough, taught enough, and given enough workshops, seminars, and consultations. I wanted solitude, and this time I wanted it forever.

A friend responded. He had an old shack on the far end of a remote wooded property with an outhouse. He said I could live there for nothing. There, in the forest, nobody would disturb me—ever. Perfect, I thought. There were only a few hitches: no water, no electricity, no heat. Never mind, I told myself. Swami Sivanandaji stood in the icy Ganges up to his neck every day from 3:00 A.M. reciting 108 malas of his mantra. This wouldn't be half as bad.

I gave away everything I owned that had an electrical cord attached: blender, iron, hot pot, one-burner, typewriter. I invested heavily in things like a manual grinder for flour, ghee lamps for night lights, all shapes of flashlights, heavy woolen socks, and Eskimo sleepwear. I said goodbye to my friends and to the world, and I moved in. The going wasn't easy. Every day, I carried five gallons of water up a steep hill. While I carried them I thought of Swami Sivananda standing in the icy Ganges (somehow that comforted me) and of the words to my favorite Sanskrit hymn:

Mano Buddhi Ahankara, Chittani Naham
Nacha Srotra Jihve, Nacha Ghrana Netre
Nacha Vyoma Bhumir Na Tejo Na Vayu
Chidananda Rupa, Shivoham, Shivoham

I am neither ego nor reason, neither mind nor thought.
I cannot be heard or cast into words, nor by smell nor sight, ever caught.
In light and wind I am not found, nor yet in earth and sky.
Consciousness and joy incarnate, Bliss of the Blissful am I.

The bliss did not come through while I was washing clothes, which I thought would surely make me a saint—or a sinner. When I shut off the kerosene heater, water froze fast, and the soaking clothes froze in it. I had never known that frozen clothes could look and feel as hard as stone. Drying them—well, I'd rather not talk about it. As for towels and sheets—I'd rather not talk about that either. Meditation, though, went well. A season passed. One day my friend asked whether I wanted to stay. "Sure," I told him. He looked surprised. "After all," I said, "the deepest experiences occur in solitude. Why should I leave? *God forbid, I might miss something.*"

One February night at 9:00 P.M., I sensed that the shack was getting colder. I checked the heater. The tank was almost full but nothing was happening. I put the switch on "high." Nothing happened. The outside thermometer read seven degrees fahrenheit. I had no vehicle. My friend had gone away with his family. The shop where I had bought the heater had closed. Options were few: heat-producing yoga breathing exercises, an all-night meditation (I don't feel the cold when I meditate), or an early, short sleep. I tried them all. When I lay down I had all my clothing on as usual— long johns, heavy trousers, jacket, woolen gloves, headgear, footgear, and even a face cover.

At 3:00 A.M. I sat up. My fingers felt stiff. Slowly, I walked down from the loft, filled my backpack with bare necessities, put more socks on my feet and on my hands, sprinkled cayenne pepper into them, and walked out. The time was 4:00 A.M. The temperature was three degrees.

I walked through the woods and out onto an icy dirt road past farm houses. Never had I known such a cold night. It seemed as though the cold had frozen all nature into stillness. Even the dogs that always barked at the slightest sound were silent. Yet the cold stillness seemed alive with sacred meaning.

Soon I turned right onto a paved road. To keep my

circulation moving I swung my arms. I was walking towards the nearest truck stop, six miles from the shack. Three hours later I reached the warm truck-stop restaurant. The sun was high in the sky then, and it streamed into the room through the frosted windows. The fresh coffee smelled good. I sat in a booth in the back of the restaurant and ordered a cup. "To the Sadguru within," I thought, as I took my first sip. No one had to tell me, "Your time in solitude is up. You've done your stint. 'Solitude forever' is not meant for you." I knew it with undeniable certainty.

I moved back into the world. Out went the manual grinder, the ghee lamps, the Eskimo sleepwear, and the silence. Within two weeks I had started a series of workshops on meditation and spiritual dynamics. Back came the blender, the iron, and the typewriter. Forty days later I completed the first draft of *Wisdom, Bliss, and Common Sense*. Now another book is in progress.

More things were taught to me on that icy morning than I had learned in solitude. I had known them, of course, for a long, long time. But we do not learn vertically. We learn spirally. The same lessons hit us over and over again before they strike home. On that six-mile walk they struck home:

Nothing is given to you for yourself—neither talents, energy, time, nor solitude. For life is not an individual affair.

When solitude is needed, solitude will happen. When action is needed, action will happen.

You have no claim to the fruits of your actions, neither to the bliss of a meditation nor to the success of a workshop.

Now that *Wisdom, Bliss, and Common Sense* is ready to be published, I have to add one more phrase: *Nor, of course, to the written book.*

xxiii

Acknowledgments

I shall always be grateful to Sri Swami Krishnananda-ji for waking me up from a long deep sleep of ignorance and imbuing me with a yearning for liberation. Many of his teachings are expressed in this book. I am grateful to the many other sages, masters, mystics, and teachers whom I had the privilege to serve and under whose guidance I studied throughout India, Nepal, Burma, Europe, South Africa, and the United States. Some have left the body in recent years. All have contributed a different dimension to my spiritual development and, ultimately, to *Wisdom, Bliss, and Common Sense.* Among them are:

Ananda Moi Ma
John C. Bennett
Sri Swami Chidananda
Raihana Ben Joybji
Mother Krishnabai
Sri Swami Lakshmanju
Sri Baba Muktananda
Padre Pio
Reverend Lama Serkong Rimpochen
Sri Jagadguru Shankaracharya

I am grateful to the directors of the Sri Aurobindo Ashram and the Ramana Maharshi Ashram in Tamil Nadu, India; to the Sayadaw Vipassana Buddhist Center in Rangoon that opened its doors during the closed season to teach a class of one; to the many Trappist, Franciscan, Carmelite, and Augustinian monks and nuns—in mission stations of the East, in the Drakensberg Mountains of South Africa, in the Catskills, Adirondacks, and Blue Ridge Mountains of the United States—who allowed me to meditate in the silence of their hermitages, knowing that I was "different," that I lived, not according to the spirit of their letter, but according to the letter of the Spirit as it unfolded in me.

1

Getting out of Your Own Way

Adversity:
A Double-Sided Coin

Fred came in a wheelchair to my workshop, "Adversity and the Spiritual Way." A drug-related accident in his mid-thirties had disabled him for life. Thin and almost bald, he looked older than his forty years. His voice was soft, and he looked down as he spoke.

"I came to ask whether you think there truly is a higher Hand behind everybody's suffering."

D. Personal experience has taught me that there is no such thing as a real "accident" and that behind whatever happens to us is a plan.

Twenty years ago, Norman Cousins, then editor of *Saturday Review,* was invited to a conference in the Soviet Union. On his last night in Moscow, he was asked to attend a reception at 5:00 P.M. about forty miles outside the city. At 3:30, a driver who picked him up either had the wrong directions or could not follow the right ones. At 6:00, Cousins was still riding on open country roads eighty miles from Moscow. Adding to his frustration was the driver's refusal to pick up speed.

---

*Questions and answers in this book are based on actual workshops given by the author. Names of all participants and their personal data have been altered to conceal their identities.

Cousins arrived four hours late. The suppressed rage that he felt during those hours caused havoc to his body. When he arrived back in the United States, he landed in the hospital with an "incurable" illness. His condition deteriorated until he realized that because negative emotions had taken such a drastic toll on his health, positive emotions might reverse his condition. He moved out of the hospital to a hotel room where he ate unprocessed food, slept without being interrupted, and watched shows like *Candid Camera* and the Marx Brothers. After every bout of laughter, his sedimentation rate dropped, and other symptoms abated. Soon he recovered, returned to work, and wrote *Anatomy of an Illness*.

Whenever I think of that Moscow driver, I cannot help feeling that a larger purpose lay behind his seeming ineptitude and his refusal to step on the gas. It seems that he merely played a role in the cosmic drama, that behind the frustrations that he caused Norman Cousins lay a Design to spread the knowledge of the causal link between mind and body. The book that emerged from Cousins's experience has shown many people how to take responsibility for their health.

F. Cousins clearly went through that suffering for a larger purpose, but I don't know if my suffering has a purpose like that. What interests me, however, is that you chose the example of his book. My real reason for coming here was an inner urge to write my story, but I don't know whether it's conceit or something deeper that motivates me.

D. Can you share it with us?

F. For two years after my accident, I indulged in self-pity. For the next two years, I condemned myself. One morning when I got up, the word "suicide" flashed through my mind.

"Oh no!" I thought. "Not that! I don't want to commit suicide!" But all day long, the thought bounced in and out of my head. By dinner time, I'd worked out the details. It felt like some outer entity was beckoning me, but I was scared to talk to anybody about it.

At 9:00 P.M., my doorbell rang. It was a young guy with a backpack. He was hitching rides to California, and he wanted directions to the local camping grounds near here. I don't know what got into me because I was never kind to strangers, but I told him he could sleep on my sofa if he wanted to.

The guy unloaded his backpack on the living-room floor, and he went to take a shower. On top of his clothes were a few books. One had a picture of Swami Sivananda on the cover, but I didn't know what a swami was. Absentmindedly, I thumbed through some pages. Still running around in my head were the details of the suicide. Suddenly, my eyes fixed on a passage. I felt as if the Swami himself transfixed them. As long as I live, I'll never forget those words.

> There is something dearer than wealth, dearer than family, dearer than life. That dearest something is your own Self, the Indweller of all beings. That all-pervading Essence is hidden in all names and forms like butter in milk and electricity in a wire. That inner Self whom the mind does not know but who knows the mind is your higher Self, Pure Consciousness. Attainment of That is called Self-Realization. That is the goal of human birth.

So much force came out of those words that I read them over and over. When I laid the book down, I was a different man from the one who had picked it up. The hitchhiker let me keep it, and he gave me another one by the swami on spiritual practices. Next day, I began to do simple yoga postures that involved only the upper part of the body. Then I started breathing exercises. Soon I started concentration and meditation according to the swami's instructions.

One evening I had been meditating for a half hour. My body got still, like a statue. Something was going on inside of me, but I didn't know what. It felt as if petals of a flower were standing straight up in the middle of my chest. Next thing I knew, I wasn't "me" anymore. I mean, I wasn't a "man" or a "person." The boundaries of what I thought was "Fred" dissolved. Suddenly I was everywhere, all at once. I was Pure Awareness, Is-Ness, Be-ing. *I was Light.* So free! The only freedom I have ever known. Nothing bound me, no body, nothing. I was complete, whole, even without my legs! Legs were nothing, and I was everything!

The experience lasted maybe minutes and maybe seconds. I don't know because time had no place there. It just stood still. Afterward, I sat motionless for a long time. Even if I had wanted to move, I couldn't. I thought back to my drug years when I was chasing after crumbs. Here I was at an emperor's feast! I was the emperor, *and the feast came out of me!*

That experience never came back, but it's okay. That one dip changed me for life.

When I look back at what happened to me—the accident, the loss of the use of my legs, the hitchhiker's visit, and Swami Sivananda's book—I can't help feeling that a Superhuman Intelligence was in back of it all. Maybe that's conceit, but if it isn't, I would like to write my story.

D. Your urge to write your story is far from conceit. You could inspire many people who do not know the purpose and value of human life. Perhaps you had to suffer to provide this inspiration for others. After all, we are an integral part of a Whole. Every change in

6

the consciousness of an individual alters the entire skein of Universal Consciousness.

It seems to me that your story carries three vital messages. One is that the purpose of human birth is the attainment of Self-Realization, a state of being in which we know we are limitless Consciousness, existence and bliss that is never affected by what happens to our body. Your second message is your apperception that a Universal Intelligence is running this cosmic panorama, for its own purposes. Your third message is that *adversity is a double-sided coin.*

Anger:
Coping on the Spot

Belle came to my workshop called "Conquest of Anger." Her desire to conquer anger stemmed from her frustrating job. Spiritual dynamics did not interest her. She had no desire to meditate, pray, or read anything but novels. Belle worked on a team that cleaned residential homes. A senior team member who apparently resented newcomers was picking on her. She watched her work, criticized, and assigned her tedious tasks, such as moving and replacing bric-a-brac. That infuriated Belle, but because expressing her fury meant losing her job, she suppressed her rage.

"Some weeks ago, I saw a television show in which a group of doctors showed slides of the inside of the human body in a state of anger. They showed how rage causes cancer. When I saw that show, I knew I had to get another job or find a better way to cope with this one."

D. I will share with you a physical, mental, and spiritual way to cope with anger on the spot. The physical approach entails simple actions. First, as soon as you sense the first ripple of irritability—I speak here not of the state of rage but of your very first sniff of its heat—nip it in the bud. Leave the scene instantly.

Head anywhere, to the bathroom, outdoors, anywhere you can be alone. Second, drink as much cold water as you can. Third, as soon as you are alone, sit down and chant out loud, or if you cannot do that, chant mentally: "Om peace. Om peace. Om peace." Prolong the "m" sound, not the vowel. The sound of "Om" will cool down your body and mind and bring you inner peace. Combine it with your breath. As you inhale, chant Om, feeling that you are inhaling peace. As you exhale, chant Om, feeling that Om is a huge broom that is sweeping all the rage out of your system.

Next, pray for the woman who made you angry.

B. Pray for her? Why should I? I can't stand her!

D. Why do you pray for anything?

B. I don't, except when I want something badly.

D. What do you want on your job?

B. I want her to leave me alone. I want her to treat me like a decent human being.

D. I am telling you how to do it. I am handing you a key that will give you exactly what you want. But you are resisting.

B. You told me to pray for her. How can I pray for somebody I don't like?

D. Whatever we want carries a price tag. When you want a pair of stockings, you have to come up with the tab. You can't get it free. If you want a job as a typist, you have to learn how to type. If you want to change this woman's behavior towards you, you have to pay the price.

B. What's the price?

D. You have to swallow a pill. The pill is called "ego."

B. How?

D. By praying.

B. How?

D. Simply say: Lord, whoever you are, whatever you

are, wherever you are, give this woman inner peace now—as much as you can. Give her good health and long life.

B. What will that do? It seems naive. How in the world would that prayer make her change towards me?

D. Thought is matter; it matters. Thoughts have color, rates of vibration, energy, direction, and influence. You have the mistaken idea that when you think of someone your thought stays with you. That's not so. Thought acts like a battery. The chemical action of a battery stays inside of it, but its dynamic correlate, an electrical current, goes out. Every thought you have has a dynamic correlate: it goes precisely where you send it!

Let us simplify this by saying that thought is energy. Energy does things. It carries out whatever intention you give it. In fact, energy is "intention in motion." It never stays home! Thought force, thought current, or mental power—whatever you want to call it—is a potent force. As soon as you think, "I hate that woman," she gets the message. What does she send back? Hate.

I am giving you a method that will change her. In the process it will change you, too. When you pray for her peace, good health, and long life, you are not merely halting the devastating effects of anger on your body. You are influencing the electromagnetic force fields of that woman's mind. This will change her behavior towards you, and will influence her to return respect and love, precisely what you want. Once you realize how much power lies within you to heal others as well as yourself, the ego pill will not taste so bitter.

B. I still don't understand how it works.

D. Have you ever seen one of those filmy hair nets that elderly women wear after they get their hair done? Touch one part of it, and the whole net moves. Similarly, our thoughts and actions constantly alter the fine, shifting tissue of energy that pervades the universe. Think ugly, and an ugly movement follows. Think love, and love follows. That's the law. We are not punished *for* what we do, but *by* what we do. The same law that governs mechanics and physics also governs the dynamics of human behavior. Every action has an equal and corresponding reaction. We can reject the law, of course. But our rejection is as meaningless as rejecting the law of gravity. It will influence our lives no matter what we believe.

Learn how to relax. Find moments alone at home, preferably on an empty stomach, to sit still. Calm your breath. Then take a self-snapshot. Ask yourself these questions: "Is my mind pulling me like an untrained puppy pulls on a leash—every way but forward? Do I follow it like a blinkered slave?" Watch your mind. You are not the mind. The more relaxed you are, the easier it is to witness what is going on in your mental factory. Patterns of mind established in your childhood may be chasing you like shadows, and perhaps nobody ever taught you how to catch them in the act.

Deepen your relaxation through the words "Om peace." One day, in a calm state, you will grasp the fact that you *are* peace, that you have never been anything else. You will see how your mental and emotional shadows obscure the peace and bliss residing in your heart. There in your heart, lie all the peace and beauty you seek outside. Once you taste deep relaxation, you will want to dive even deeper through meditation. When you start meditating, not only will *you* transform. Everybody around you will change with no intentional effort on your part.

B. Why should relaxing and meditating bring about those changes?

D. We are transformers. We take in one kind of

energy and give out another. On a physical level, energies include air, sunlight, water, and food. Around our subtle bodies is a subtler, more potent replenishing power, a constant Presence from which we derive peace, force, and light, but only when we are receptive to it. Without hospitality, we are like three-dollar pocket radios trying to pick up Radio Beijing.

In your spare moments, you might reflect on two profound statements. The first is what Sri Swami Sivananda said to an angry person whose boss had called him a fool: "If a man calls you a fool, why should you get so upset and prove that he is right?" The second was stated by the late master psychologist, Carl Jung: "What we cannot forgive in others is what we cannot forgive in ourselves."

Anger:
Eastern Keys to Mastery

Problems with gout, high blood pressure, and his heart marred the retirement years that Boyd had looked forward to. During his adult life, he had worked on computers, creating software for financial institutions. Now, urged by his doctor, Boyd was working on himself. "Either I master anger," he told us, "or I won't make it to the end of this year."

When the pastor of Boyd's church sponsored a senior citizens' workshop in relaxation and meditation, Boyd and his wife participated. During the first session, he felt as if somebody had taken a ton of weight off his shoulders. Tears welled up, and he had to walk outside where he could cry out alone. Since then, Boyd and his wife have gone to several self-transformation workshops.

"Tracy and I used to think that what we wanted most was an around-the-world cruise on an ocean liner. Not anymore. What we're after now is inner experience.

"My problem is anger, and it comes up all the time. Yesterday afternoon I was taking a nap when somebody knocked on our door. The guy tried to sell me insurance. If there is anything I don't want any more of, it's insurance! I felt like killing him for waking me up. That's only one example but it happens a lot. I want to learn how to conquer my anger before I leave this mortal frame."

D. Vedic, Buddhist, and Christian traditions offer several means of conquering anger that we can group under three computer modes: delete, control, and insert.

Let's look at "delete." Eastern spiritual masters say that deleting flesh foods is essential for the conquest of anger. In *The Chakras*, author C. W. Leadbeater states that meat coarsens the body. The Vedic tradition explains why: The cosmic quality of "tamas" or heaviness pervades flesh foods. As we eat, so we are. These foods increase the propensities inherent in the lower part of our bodies—inertia, anger, and sexual drive. Garlic, onions, and alcohol also heat and stimulate the body and increase its propensity for anger.

Hormones, tranquilizers, antibiotics, and other drugs given to livestock before they are born, while they live, and after they die, cause additional hazards in the human bloodstream. These and other chemicals trigger high levels of stress which tend to induce disease, anger, and fear. Added to all this are the toxic effects of glandular secretions that animals inject into their bloodstream in a state of hostility and fear—and what we eat, we become. To keep our bodies and minds healthy, light and peaceful, we need to eat foods that are natural conductors of fine energy—dairy foods, vegetables, grains and fruit.

Another item under "delete" is indiscriminate television viewing. What goes in must come out. An intake of violence means an output of violence. Films and pictures that stimulate memories of sex also can trigger anger, for it is said that lust is the reverse side of the coin of anger.

Let's look at the "control" mode of mastery. Energy losses can trigger anger, and we lose energy when we talk a lot. Spiritual masters advise aspirants to observe silence for several hours a day and periodically, to spend a whole day in silence.

Under the "insert" mode are three suggestions: simple Hatha Yoga postures to regulate hormonal secretions, make your body strong, and calm your nerves; pranayama exercises to quiet your breath and mind; meditation and self-inquiry on "Who Am I" to free you from thinking that you are your emotions. Identifying with your Essence and Consciousness within instead of your feelings will help you to regain your control.

George Ivanovitch Gurdjieff, the "rascal sage," said that most of us are like machines on automatic pilot. Like ping-pong balls, we feel great when life goes well, and we are down when the going gets tough. Everything "happens" to us. Love happens—hate, desire, anger. We live and act as if we were effects. Yet we are Cause Itself! Transmuting the energy of anger through these practices will free us from the ping-pong syndrome. We begin to ride our horse instead of letting our horse ride us. This state of consciousness is what we are looking for.

B. That is what I need to conquer anger?

D. Not the words. You need action. Translating into action even half of these suggestions is more than enough for self-mastery.

B. Suppose somebody comes along who grates on my nerves like a bad floppy disc. What then?

D. If your spiritual computer is in good shape, it will eject the disc. If it is not, you can mull over this statement by a great Western psychologist: "We never see people as *they* are. We always see people as *we* are."

15

B. I can accept that idea when another guy grates on me, but suppose that all the abuse and anger come from him and not from me.

D. In that case, you can think about the Buddha. He was lecturing in a village square one evening when a villager approached him and began to abuse him. The Buddha said to him: "If you hand me a piece of paper and I refuse to accept it, what happens to the paper?" The villager said, "It stays with me."

"That is precisely what I am doing with your abuse," said the Buddha. "I am *not* taking it. Your abuse remains with you!"

Anger:
You Have a Right
Not To Be Angry

Solly brought his anger to my workshop on "Conquest of Anger." He worked for the marketing department of one of America's top ten corporations. He described his job as "pushing retailers to push our product." With heated speech and gestures, he told us that he knew anger was unhealthy. "How many times have I heard that! But still, life goes on. A month ago, my boss promoted a young woman to a spot senior to mine. The woman has half my experience. Now she earns twice my salary. When that happened, I blew up, and I've been steaming since. Yes, anger may be bad, it's true, but in this case I have a *right* to be angry! Do you agree?"

D. A young woman in a town where I used to live had a heated fight with her husband one morning before he left for work. They exchanged violent words. He slammed the door and walked out, and she cursed him out loud for an hour. In that mood of extreme rage, she breast-fed her three-month-old baby. A few hours later, the baby turned blue. By evening the baby was dead.

In a state of anger, injurious toxins are secreted by the glands and injected into the bloodstream. *Your*

17

bloodstream, not your boss's. When you are angry, your white blood cell count plummets. That lower count can deal the death blow to your immune system. *Your* immune systems, not his. Anger shortens *your* life, nobody else's. Anger is suicide, not homicide. Now do you see why you have a right *not* to be angry?

Attachment:
Hold it Lightly

Dressed elegantly, middle-aged Roslyn looked younger than her years. She came to my workshop on "Growing in the Spiritual Life" along with her children—a nineteen-year-old daughter who had an Indian guru and a seventeen-year-old son who practiced Zen meditation. When Roslyn's husband died a year ago, her children taught her to meditate. Since then she experienced an inner quietude and a calm joy that she had not known before. She now wanted to "go deeper," but her children told her that attachments held her back.

"I have many fine artifacts in my home, and I love them all," Roslyn said. "My children tell me that I must get rid of them if I want to make spiritual progress. But I can't do it, and frankly, I see no harm in keeping them. Am I wrong, or are they wrong?"

D. All traditions speak of the proverbial bird that can not fly because its wings are tied to a post. Sages say that a wing is held down as much by a thin silk thread as it is by a heavy rope. So we must give up attachments if we are to progress. What should go is the *attachment* to objects, not necessarily the objects themselves. How would getting rid of your artifacts benefit you now? You would still carry them in your mind. Positive or negative attachments held in our minds keep us back just as surely as the things themselves.

A tale from the East makes an interesting point about this. Two celibate monks were walking along a forest path. One was old and one was young. When they reached a stream they removed their sandals to cross it barefoot. Just then, they saw a beautiful woman. She was crying because the open sores on her feet prevented her from walking barefoot. Immediately, the older monk bent down, lifted her up in his arms, and carried her across the stream. The younger monk followed in astonishment. After the older one let the woman down on the other side of the stream, the two monks walked a long way in silence. Three hours later, the younger monk could stand it no longer.

"What you did was shocking!" he blurted out. The older monk looked surprised. "What are you talking about?" he asked.

"You carried that beautiful woman in your arms. And you know, Brother, we are celibates!"

The older monk burst out laughing. "Imagine!" he said. "The moment I put the woman down, I completely forgot about her. But you have been carrying her with you for three whole hours! Which one of us has the attachment?"

Keep your artifacts but learn to hold them lightly by deepening your meditation on Truth. If you practice regularly, and if you already feel a constant quiet joy, then soon you may experience waves of bliss that will make the joys of the world seem like toys. Once the bliss of the Supreme touches you, your equilibrium will not be shaken by the presence or absence of anything in the world. Then life's greatest lesson will govern your life: "Hold it lightly!"

Attachment:
From Ownership
to Stewardship

Walter came to my workshop on "The Dynamics of Spiritual Growth." For fifty years, he had worked as a house painter. A retiree, a widower, and a grandfather of six, he wanted to prepare himself for "the inevitable." "I'm ashamed to say this," he said. "Here I am, an old man who can count the years he has left. What makes me sad is having to leave the things I own like bowling trophies and pictures of my family. And my grandkids—I don't even dare think about leaving them. I know I can't take anything with me. While I am still alive, I would like to get a little more detached from all that. How does an old man start walking on that road to freedom?"

D. Because you called it "the road to freedom," I'd say you are already well on your way. As I see it, nobody owns anything. We human beings do not own homes, property, money, furniture, cars, or clothes. We do not own even our time, energy, skills, looks, health, or anything else inside or outside of us. That realization can come as a shock. But when it comes, we are free. Are your trophies the rotating kind?

W. A few are. Others have my name inscribed on them.

21

D. The ones that rotate are a good starting point. When you look at them, what do you think?

W. I think that they are nice to have while I have them but I know that they are not mine to keep as they'll move on to the next winner.

D. Beautifully said. Everything you have in your home and in your body is a rotating trophy. Nice to have around while you have it, but not yours to keep. Ownership is fiction. *Stewardship* is truth. You and I and everybody else on earth are stewards of everything we think we possess. Anything and anyone can be taken from us at any time. We are stewards even of our lives.

So the road to freedom for you, whether you are old or young, is the exercise of looking at everything in your life as a rotating trophy—not just the good stuff but the bad stuff too. Every bit of it is temporary. As you look at everything and everybody, even your reflection in the mirror, think of your real Self as a river bank. Water flows relentlessly between your long great arms. You let it flow and splash your sides, and you enjoy its touch, but never do you stretch out your arms to grab it for keeps.

Whatever is given to us we should use well, without saying or thinking, ''This is mine, good, bad, delightful, painful.'' Such expressions imply relationship. Objects are not bad in themselves; it is the relationship that we establish with them that constitutes our bondage. What you are trying to do in becoming detached is to place a different value on your external world. Whenever you become aware of clinging, remind yourself that you don't *own* anything; that your grandchildren come in and out of your life like figures on a movie screen; that your trophies and pictures can be stolen, damaged, and gone from your life forever; that everything your senses perceive, including your body, are transitory phenomena. Realize that the reality and meaning of all these things lies only in the value that you imbue them with.

Once I knew a woman who was constantly preoccupied with her beauty. For hours every day, she massaged, creamed, and mud-packed her face and massaged her hair and scalp with fine oils. Mirrors in all her rooms served as reminders and affirmations of her beauty. For some months, I did not see her. When we met again at a shopping mall, I barely recognized her. She had been in a car accident. A dozen plastic surgery operations had not restored a fraction of her original beauty. The loss devastated her, but the devastation brought her to the spiritual life. That is a tough way to learn the lesson of stewardship.

The Bible puts it well: "Lay not your treasures where they will rust." You might put aside a little time every day to look deeply into that non-rotating Trophy that will never rust.

Desires:
Scratching the Itch

Mandy followed a pathless path. For ten years she meditated regularly, but not on a deity or on the Impersonal Reality. She focused on herself, trying to see through the deceptions of her mind.

"It strikes me that desire is the biggest thorn in our flesh," she said. "It blinds us and keeps us running. A while ago I went to your workshop on 'Paths to Self-Realization.' You said something about desires that I can't forget. You quoted an Indian master who said that our distance from God is directly proportionate to the number of desires we have.

"Recently, I have been watching my mind closely. Desires pop up and carry me away before I know it. It happens like a push-button machine. A desire rises, a green light flashes, my legs move, or my mind schemes. It seems as if 'nobody is home' to intervene. Can you share your understanding of this?"

D. The master in India whom you referred to was lecturing one morning to a group of foreigners. He saw a young man at the back of the room pick up a back-scratcher and scratch his back.

"What are you doing?" he asked him.

"Scratching an itch," the young man said.

24

"Does it feel good?" the Master asked. The young man nodded.

"Why?"

"Scratching an itch is always a nice feeling," the young man said.

"It is not the act of scratching that gives you a good feeling," the master corrected. "You feel good because *scratching makes the itch go away!*"

Desires itch. They keep us on the go. As each one clamors for our attention, we seek ways to gratify it. Satisfaction brings temporary peace. But peace does not come from objects; peace comes from getting rid of the desire! Seldom do we realize that peace lies only in the brief span of time between the cessation of one desire and the rise of another. The longer the time span between two desires, the more peace we feel. Peace is inversely proportionate to the frequency of desire. Peace is the "space" between thoughts. Peace is the trough between waves. Peace is the off-cycle, the silent counterpart of a sound wave. Peace is a state of being in which the mind is still.

M. What is the effect of gratifying desires as they come up?

D. Gratifying desires to get rid of them is like throwing kerosene on a fire to put it out. Satisfaction fuels desire. Every indulgence perfects our automatic cycle: itch-scratch-satisfy, itch-scratch-satisfy, itch-scratch-satisfy. The cycle makes us restless. It turns our attention away from the only real peace.

M. What is the alternative response?

D. Sri Ramana Maharshi says that when desire arises in the mind, we should face it squarely and ask: To whom does this desire occur? Who perceives it? The act of asking and witnessing will cut through the mechanical cycle. *It will bring our consciousness back to center, back to what we truly are.* If we do not break the

25

cycle this way or with a similar de-brain-washing practice, we live like an untrained puppy that pulls its leash in every direction but forward.

The Indian master also said that the entire universe is an embodiment of want. I think of the world as a bowling ball. Desire sticks its three fingers into the ball and imbues it with a strong momentum of intention. With that momentum, the ball is flung onto the alley, geared to hit the tenpin objects of sense.

Our goal in life is not the tenpins. Our goal is freedom from desire. The path to freedom lies in not identifying with the waves of the mind. You are quite right. Desires keep us hopping until we can hop no more, and with good reason: we never get enough of what we don't really want.

Ego:
The Fatal Sense of Do-ership

Wendy studied music in a community college where she also led a weekly class on yoga and meditation for fellow students. Before going to college, she had lived in an ashram studying yoga and Eastern music with an American swami.

"This whole business of 'I,' 'me,' 'mine'—'culprits' our swami called them—has me confused. Last week I handed a paper to my English professor. It came back dotted with red marks. He wrote, 'Too many I's. Consider: do they fill your speech, too?'

"I began to listen to how I talk. Sure enough, he was right. 'I think, I will, I do, I believe; I want, I don't want, I predict, I know. . . .' Everytime I speak, it comes out. There it goes again! What can I do?"

D. In certain ashrams, seekers practice speaking without the word "I." Instead of saying, "I see a car," they would say, "These eyes are seeing a car," which is much more to the point. Or, as Sri Nisargadatta advises in *I Am THAT,* you can say, "A car is being seen." Somebody who corresponds with me writes letters that do not have one single "I" in them, so it is possible. Take your professor's critique to heart, and see whether you can get your points across without the word "I." Try it for a few assignments, and see what happens. The challenge is fascinating.

W. Our swami taught us only simple yoga and simple meditation. He did not go into the philosophy very much. So apart from the annoying sound of the constant "I," I really don't understand what's wrong with the word.

D. Nothing is wrong with it. It just lacks reality.

W. If there is no "I," then who is doing everything?

D. There is One Supreme Being. Through the power of self-expression, this Being manifests as many. We are those expressions. You may call it instruments, vehicles, even limbs of the Divine. The point is that there is One Supreme Entity, not a plurality of entities. So the more we think in terms of "I", the more out of tune we are with Truth.

W. That sounds too theoretical for me. I'm a musician. I need to think in terms of experience, not theories. What, for example, would a woman who knew she had no separate "I" be like? How would she differ from somebody who didn't know it?

D. This story may answer your question.

Savitri came from a low-caste family in East India. From the time she was eight years old, she felt an intense love for Lord Krishna. Every morning she worshipped him at the family altar, and all day long she thought of him.

As was the custom in her culture, an early marriage was arranged for her. Savitri did not want to marry, for Lord Krishna was her only beloved. The worst part of it was that she would wed a fisherman, she who could never hurt any creature no matter how lowly. She would even have to sell his fish.

This distressed her very much and one morning she cried at the altar to Sri Krishna. Suddenly, she heard his voice: "You are my beloved child, Savitri. Do not fear. I am placing you in unclean circumstances so you may glorify me. Your feet will walk in mud, but like a lotus, your head will breathe the air of purity."

"But Lord," Savitri sobbed, "I want to love only you! I want no other."

Sri Krishna said, "In your husband, you will see me alone. In the buyers of fish, you will see only me. In the fish themselves, you will perceive me. The day will come when you and I will merge. The boundaries of Savitri will dissolve, and you will know that it is your Lord Krishna alone who lives and acts through the form you call 'Savitri!' "

The wedding day came. When the ritualistic rice and saffron were placed upon her head, Savitri thought in her heart, "I am marrying Lord Krishna. His Supreme Majesty gazes upon me through the inert eyes of this husband-form. He alone shall I serve as long as I live."

Soon Savitri began to sell her husband's fish. People liked to buy from her because of her resplendent peace and joy. If they felt depressed when they came in, they felt cheerful when they left.

One day, a high-caste woman named Padma moved near the fishery. Padma observed all the rules. She never ate flesh foods, never lied, stole, or killed even an insect, that is, not until the Friday afternoon when a huge flying cockroach landed on her kitchen floor. Without thinking, she crushed it with her foot.

"Oh!" she cried. "Look what I have done! I have killed a cockroach! Now I shall surely go to hell." Padma scooped up the creature, wrapped it in a small cloth, and went out in search of a way to save her soul.

As she passed the fishery she saw Savitri, whom she considered unclean because she touched and sold dead fish. Then Padma got an idea. Since Savitri was already sullied, what would it matter if she took the blame for killing the roach? She went in. "Look what I did!" she told Savitri. "In my whole life I never killed a thing. But a few minutes ago I killed a cockroach!"

Savitri smiled. "Don't fear, Padma," she said gently. "Give the cockroach to me. I will take your mistake from you." Padma was overjoyed, and she dropped the dead insect into Savitri's hand. "Thank you, Savitri! Thank you!" she cried.

"I am happy to serve you," said Savitri.

Many years later, both women died and were cremated on the same day. Ascending to a subtle plane, they met the Keeper of the Middle-Gate. The gate led to two elevators. The right one went up, and the left one led to the basement. The Gate-Keeper took out the files of both women and checked their accounts. "Padma," he said, "You will go through the door on your left and take the elevator to the basement. You, Savitri, will go through the right door and take the elevator to the top."

Padma raged. "That's impossible!" she shouted. "Impossible! In my whole life, I've never done anything wrong—except for killing one cockroach. This woman, Savitri, sold dead fish. She made cemeteries of peoples' stomachs. *She* is the one who should go to the basement, not I! I am destined to go up!"

Again the keeper checked his records. "Sorry, Padma," he said. "It says here that when Savitri sold the dead fish she *knew* that she, her husband, her customers, and each fish she touched were nothing but the forms of her beloved Lord Krishna. She saw all her actions and thoughts as the Lord's. She never had the sense that she, Savitri, was a separate agent of her actions. But when you stepped on that cockroach, your first thought was, 'Oh! Look what I have done! I, Padma, have killed a cockroach!' "

The Keeper handed Padma her pass. Sobbing hysterically, she read it: "Basement Pass for Padma—Purchased for the Price of *Ego—The Fatal and Fictitious Sense of Do-ership.*"

Fear of Death:
A Powerful Antidote

Clyde drove 150 miles to attend my workshop, "Death and Dying: An Eastern Perspective." Laughter, music, and family noise had filled his house for four decades. The house quieted down when the children left to start families of their own. Then his wife died and overnight the home he had loved became a cemetery—no music, no laughter, no one to fix breakfast, wash his clothes, make the bed, or ask how he felt.

"So this is death, I began to think. Living death. Walking from room to room like a zombie, I thought about real death. What would it be like? Life, snuffed out in an instant like a candle. The flame burns for a moment. Then, nothing. Only darkness. That scares me, the thought of the final end of it all. I tried to stop thinking of it. I even went to parties at the senior citizens' center. But the thought of death never left the back of my mind. Now it's more than a thought. Now I'm caught in the grip of fear, scared of the instant when it will suddenly be all over."

D. Often our fears come as blessings in disguise. Let me share a true story of someone who had the same fear.

When Sri Ramana Maharshi was sixteen years old,

31

he was struck one day by a violent fear of death. The fear was inexplicable because he was not ill. Yet he heard himself think, "I am going to die! I'm going to die!" The thought of a doctor never occurred to him because he was not sick. So overpowering was his fear of death that it drove his mind inwards. "Death has come," he told himself. "What does it mean?"

He lay on the floor and stretched his limbs out stiffly as though rigor mortis had set in. He imitated a corpse in every way he could. He held his breath and thought, "Now this body is dead. Soon it will be carried stiff to the cremation ground, burnt and reduced to ashes. But with the death of this body, am I dead?" he asked himself. "Is the body 'I'?"

Suddenly, he felt the full force of the "I," totally apart from his body. "Oh!" he exclaimed. "I am *not* the body! I am the Spirit that transcends it. Now I know! The body dies, but the Spirit that transcends it cannot be touched by death. That means that *I am the deathless Spirit.*" Those words flashed through him vividly as living truth that he perceived directly, even without thought. His "I" was far more real than his body. In that split instant, his fear of death vanished forever, and his absorption in the Self continued unbroken for the rest of his life.

Fear stems from alienation from the Self or God through false identification with the body. Death always frightens people who think they are the body. Yet death never affects the Self. Disintegration occurs only in the five elements that constitute the gross body—earth (hardness), water (liquidity), fire (heat), air (movement), and ether (space). We step out of these gross elements much as we would step out of a worn-out garment.

Knowing this intellectually is one thing; experiencing it is another. I suggest that you begin spiritual practices with daily study and deep reflection on the scripture *Self-Knowledge (Atma Bodha)* by Sri Adi Shankaracharya, and on the words of Sri Ramana Maharshi. Invite friends to your home, ones who suffer as you do from the agonizing fear of death, and share the readings with them. In that way, you will make the best use of the space and time available to you. When you sense an inner desire to meditate, ask a good yoga teacher for guidance. Meditation can take you beyond body consciousness. It can lead you to the experience of yourself as boundless spirit.

C. I thought that only monks had experience like that.

D. Anyone who yearns for it, and works for it, can have it. In the book *Cosmic Consciousness* Dr. Richard Bucke records transcendental experiences of people like Bacon, Blake, Whitman, Emerson, Thoreau, Swedenborg, Spinoza, and others. They were not monks; yet among their common spiritual experiences were an all-embracing light, the sense of immortality, and an instantaneous loss of fear.

For the fear of death, no antidote has more power than the knowledge of who we really are.

Guilt:
It's Never Too Late
to Make Amends

Twenty-year-old Shawn had long hair and wore a wide red band around his forehead and a gray T-shirt with the words, "The New Age Is Here." He carried a heavy load of guilt. While his father was dying of cancer, he had hung out with the drug crowd in his town. "I didn't spend enough time with him," he told us. "Now it's too late. He's dead. Is there anything I can do to appease my guilt?"

D. First of all, let us look at the word "death." Existence cannot die. Existence is eternal. No one goes beyond it. No one can pass out of it. Existence is the underlying substratum of all that is. Superimposed upon it are temporary names and forms that rise and subside like waves in the ocean. Death refers to the dissolution of the elements of the body in all their permutations, not to the being. When the elements of the body decay and can no longer express the progress of the spirit within, the Consciousness withdraws itself. If a person has not attained God-Realization in this birth, he or she will be born again and again in different forms.

S. What happens to people at death and between lives?

34

D. Spiritual masters tell us that at death, the being, enveloped by the subtle body, leaves the gross body through the head. If the being has strong attachments to people, places, and things, it may remain earthbound for a long time. Then it goes to different planes of existence where it experiences the fruits of its actions in this life. After it passes through those experiences it rests in a state of quiescence until it is time to start a new life. You can understand this process clearly through books written by C. W. Leadbeater and Annie Besant about the astral plane, the astral body, and what happens after ''death.''

In the light of this, let's take an objective look at your guilt. You are young. When you were hanging out with the drug crowd, you were even younger. What were your values in those years? What thoughts filled your mind? If you had spent more time with your father then, would your values and thoughts have helped his moods and feelings and your relationship with him? In all probability, your proximity to him at that time might have had an adverse effect.

Now is the time to contact your father. Now that your heart is open and you are channeling higher forms of energy, you can help him. He may not be clothed in a physical sheath, but he may, in fact, be sitting closer to you than the woman on your right.

Sit in the silence for some minutes every morning and evening. Relax your body, and slow down your breathing. Visualize your father if you can, and mentally repeat his first name. When all your mental static stops and you have made a clear inner contact, send him thought-waves of love and peace from the recesses of your heart. This regular practice will do more for your father's spirit than years of unenlightened conversation.

It is never too late to make amends.

A Hard Heart:
Only Softness
Perceives Hardness

Janice was the sole survivor in a car accident that killed
her husband, her mother, and her two children. Having spent many years before that repeating the mantra, "Thy will be done," she was able to accept the
trauma in a spirit of surrender. "The Lord gives, and
the Lord takes," she kept saying. After the accident
Janice began to meditate regularly. "Meditation acts
like a beam of light on my character," she said. "Every
time my mind calms down, all my vices and weak-
nesses show up—like hardness of heart. Why?"

D. When you pour a steady stream of fresh, pure
water into a bucket of dirty water, dirt will rise to the
surface and overflow. Sri Aurobindo suggests that
when you experience an impurity in yourself, you open
that area for the descent of divine force and light.
Transformation occurs through your desire for change
and your inner hospitality to that power.

The fact that you observe hardness of heart shows
that softness is there too. How else could you perceive
it? Only the changeless perceives change. Only the Infinite perceives the finite. Only softness perceives hardness. No "thing" can know itself; only something else

can know it. Recognize, then, that a higher part of your nature has observed a lower part.

Everything happens for a reason. Behind your sense of hardness of heart lies a cosmic impulse for deeper levels of transformation. In other words, you are being shown your next step. We purify and progress not for our own enhancement, but to become greater instruments of the Divine.

Impatience:
Our Words Create Our Worlds

Susan meditated twice a day to relax. As a mother of four who worked part-time in a florist shop, she had problems with high blood pressure. Meditation lowered it, but she did not know how to bring inner peace into her life.

"Today I went to a large supermarket," she said. "All I got was a loaf of bread and a carton of cigarettes. I was rushed. In a few minutes, I had to pick up my daughter at her school bus stop. I stood in the line at the express checkout. The line moved fast until an old woman in front of me got to the cashier. She turned her handbag upside down and began counting out nickels and pennies. Watching her, I felt the heat rise in my head. My brain seemed to boil. Every four-letter word in the book came into my mind. Idiot, I thought. She'll push up my pressure. I wanted to bop her on the head. By the time I got out of the store, my heart was palpitating so loudly that I had to sit still in my car before I dared drive. This kind of thing happens to me often, and I don't know how to deal with it."

D. First, it is essential to understand that the woman was in no way responsible for the rise in your blood pressure. You were. Second, your impatience and inner cursing did nothing to speed the woman up. All it did was tear you down.

Having meditated, you know that when no words arise in your mind, the mind becomes still and you experience peace. Words carry power. When words arise in your mind, powerful images rise along with them. You identify with the images. That identification evokes pleasure or pain. When we recognize this phenomenon for what it is, we cannot help but be fascinated by it: through the power of words alone, we create our inner world. Through the power of words we create our prisons. Then we spend the rest of our lives trying to get out of them. Our minds create both heaven and hell. Hell takes much more energy.

Here is a key to help you use this power for your benefit instead of your detriment. Next time you wait in line and you become aware of negative reactions in your mind, immediately substitute these words: "Patient I am. Relaxed I am," or "Om Patience, Om Peace." Repeat them over and over mentally. As you do, the feelings behind those words will manifest within you. Those feelings will keep your body processes in check. More important, you will have made the first big step in taking responsibility for your health.

We can never change the world. All we can do is change our reactions to it.

Indecision:
Every Solution
Is a Compromise

Tessa took so long to decide whether to come to my workshop that she arrived half an hour late. Her gentle features and barely audible voice conveyed the impression of a young girl; yet Tessa was thirty-two years old. Making decisions of any kind was painful for her.

"I weigh the pros and cons, and I get nowhere," she said. "When I want to attend a workshop in another town, I think about how much I want to go. Then immediately, other thoughts rush in: if I go, my husband will have to pick up our kids from school, and he'll have to cook, and so on. My mind keeps vacillating between desire and guilt or desire and fear. I've had some therapy, but it didn't help this problem. Would some spiritual practice help?"

D. Yes, but first you need to grasp two facts: you are a perfectionist, and your relentless search for perfection is pointless because perfection does not exist in the relative world. You need to contemplate and surrender to this truth.

Whenever you have to make a decision, practice this simple discipline. First, make a preliminary decision to remain undecided for twenty-four hours. Then take two sheets of paper and draw a vertical line down the

40

middle of each. Head one sheet "A" and the other "B." Above the left-hand columns, write "Pros"; above the right ones, "Cons." List all advantages and disadvantages for both A and B. Make sure that you put on paper every thought that hovers in your mind on paper. When you finish, give it no more attention and put the papers out of sight.

Before you go to bed, relax your body and still your mind as much as you can. Sit with your spine straight but with no tension in the body. Review in your mind what you wrote on paper without trying to make any decision. Your task is only to saturate your mind with the thoughts you put in writing. When you have completed your mental review, place the decision into the hands of the Universal Intelligence with this prayer of surrender: "I leave this decision in your Hands. As it is willed, so shall it be." Then drop it.

Next morning you will probably experience an inner pull in one particular direction. Accept it with whatever compromises it entails. When your mind throws up its customary doubts and vacillations, remind it of the truth that no solution is perfect. Every solution is a compromise between contradictory forces.

Soon your mind will leave you in peace.

Intoxicants:
Their Subtle Effects

Larry came from a wealthy family that disowned him in his sixteenth year when they found out he had sold their jewels to buy cocaine. Jobless and homeless for the next five years, he roamed from state to state on the east coast. He slept in doorways, bus stations, and shelters. He ate in soup kitchens and hostels. Occasionally, he picked up a job for a few days loading trucks, mowing lawns, or shoveling snow. His earnings went back into drugs.

A year ago, he met a young Episcopalian priest who, Larry said, showed him more love than he had gotten from anybody. The minister took him into his home and gave him a room, food, and clothing. In return, Larry worked around his house and their church. In the evenings, they sat together and talked about Larry's life.

"After a while, Father taught me some postures that he had learned from a book on Christian yoga. Then he taught me how to meditate. We followed a few methods in Lawrence LeShan's book, *How to Meditate*. I found great peace through that.

"Last month, Father gave me a new job: seeking seekers. He said they were out there on the streets looking for drugs to blast their minds out of existence.

He said I needed to talk to them, one on one, and to teach small groups of kids to meditate, because that's what they really want. He told me to show them how to still their minds without drugs. So that's what I am doing now. I get no money, just a small stipend, but I have hardly any needs. Not having a bank account doesn't bother me at all. The joy I get talking to kids who suffer like I did is so great that I don't need anything else.

"I came here this evening to get some help for my work. Some of the kids ask questions I can't answer. I want to know exactly what drugs and alcohol do to us, how they harm us—not the ordinary stuff that doctors and druggists and parents talk about—but other things like subtle effects. I need to know more so that I can be of more help."

D. First of all, the kids should know that they already have everything they are looking for. They want the headless, mindless experience of infinite bliss, infinite knowledge, infinite freedom. They can have it now, free, without drugs. They should know that while their bodies and minds are limited, the Self is not. Self is what they are. To know that truth—to have that experience—is the reason they meditate. Once they tap into the infinite euphoria, your work is done.

You might read them some passages from a marvelous little book that describes with great clarity the experience of enlightenment: Douglas Harding's *On Having No Head*. The spiritual experiences of other mystics will also show them what they can look forward to. Knowing where they are headed can motivate them to get there.

Yoga teaches that around the Self are three "bodies": causal, subtle, and gross. The outermost body is our gross physical body, which is composed of food. The

43

subtle body is shaped like the physical body, but because it is subtler, it interpenetrates it. It is in the subtle body that we experience the effects of drugs and all pleasure and pain. This body consists of seventeen elements: the five subtle organs of sense; the five subtle organs of action, the five pranas you have read about in yoga books; the mind; and the intellect.

In this body are a number of centers of consciousness called *chakras* in Sanskrit. Most of the higher centers are closed or partially closed. To open them is the subtle aim of spiritual practice. When they open, there is no limit to what a human being can become, for these centers contain our total potentiality. Of the many centers, seven are most important. Directly connected to the glands in the physical body, these seven centers are located at the base of the spine, the genital area, the solar plexus, the heart (center of chest), the hollow of the throat, the center of the eyebrows, and the crown of the head.

These chakras resemble lotuses. Each lotus has a different number of petals. The base of the spine has four; the genital chakra has six; the one at the navel has ten; and so on. When the centers are closed, their petals point downward. As spiritual force rises from the lower chakra in disciplines such as Kundalini or Tantric Yoga, or descends from above the head as in the yoga discipline of Sri Aurobindo, the centers open. The petals then reverse their position and point upwards like a perfect lotus, releasing inner power for transformation.

In *The Complete Illustrated Book of Yoga*, Sri Swami Vishnudevananda writes that as "Kundalini," the spiritual energy, rises from the lower nerve plexuses to the higher ones, layer after layer of mind opens, and many powers and visions come to the yogi. "When the Kundalini reaches the last and highest center, the thousand-petaled lotus in the brain, he becomes perfectly detached from his body and mind, and his soul is freed from all limitations caused by time and space. Here the yogi realizes his eternal existence and enjoys the bliss of the superconscious state.''

Except for a brief instant when intoxicants trigger a distorted movement in the centers and release euphoria, alcohol, cocaine, heroine, marijuana, and a thousand other drugs including excess caffeine depress the petals and keep them pointing downwards in an inverted position, so that they inhibit the passage of spiritual force. In such states of consciousness, we are no longer walking forward on the evolutionary path; we are headed backwards.

L. I have read about the chakras and I believe what you say about how drugs affect them. But how can I convince the kids out there of things they cannot see?

D. Only experience will convince them. But even to seek that experience, they need to be motivated by whatever tangible data you can show them. You might start by talking about the subtle body. Long ago it was understood only by mystics and clairvoyants. When Kirlian, the Russian peasant photographer, found a way to film the electrical energy associated with the subtle body, it became more widely known. (The subtle body is not only within the physical; it extends several inches beyond it.) Kirlian photos appear to reflect actual changes in this energy field around the body and around plants. You can find Kirlian photographs in reference books at most libraries. More data is available from books on psychic discoveries in the Soviet Union.

You could show the kids pictures of chakras from the book *Chakras* by the clairvoyant C. W. Leadbeater. Slides and films about the subtle body and its chakras are also available through the Theosophical Society and parapsychology institutes. If this idea interests Father, he might order films or slides and allow you to show them to the "street seekers" at the church.

L. That kind of data would intrigue the kids. With all this evidence available, why is it that most people refuse to accept these things?

D. They don't have the courage to look truth in the eye because that would mean the demise of their cherished concepts. If they could accept truth, the need for drugs would plummet. Life would be fulfilling, for self-expression rather than accrual would become our highest priority. What does the drug crave indicate? It tells us that *to have* is not what we want. What we want more than anything is *to be*.

The work you are doing is vital. You are taking kids out of a dark wasteland and leading them to light. You are showing them how to go *within*. That is what they want. For only when they go within, will they find their way out.

Jealousy:
Eastern Keys to Mastery

Jealousy troubled Virginia, a legal secretary who had recently married for the third time. "I'm jealous of my husband's time, of his freedom, of his success," she said. "It's destroying our marriage, but I can't stop it. Would some spiritual discipline help me?"

D. Three spiritual approaches can help you root out jealousy.

(1) The first method comes from Raja Yoga, the science of mental development. St. Teresa of Avila referred to this method when she said, "If you can imagine being in possession of a virtue, you are already halfway there." Cultivating the virtue opposite the one you want to get rid of is the key. In your case, you want nobility and magnanimity. Every morning and evening for twenty minutes, sit in a quiet place and relax your body. Slow down your breathing. Inhale peace and exhale tension. Begin to repeat mentally, over and over, "Om nobility. Om magnanimity," and concentrate on the meaning of the words. If you practice regularly, this method should free you from jealousy in forty days.

(2) The second method comes from Jnana Yoga or Vedanta, the way of knowledge. In this yoga, you re-

flect and meditate on yourself and others not as names and forms, but as the One indivisible limitless expanse of Consciousness and all-pervading ocean of Light. You view emotions such as lust or jealousy as coming from outside of yourself. You do not identify with them; you stand back as a perennial Witness. When you realize the Self within, you will see the same Self appearing everywhere in myriads of names and forms. That experience dissolves all sense of separation and therefore all jealousy.

(3) The third spiritual approach comes from Bhakti Yoga, the yoga of devotion. On this path you practice perceiving the Lord in all creation. You ask yourself this question: "How can I be jealous of that person when it is the Lord who acts and speaks through him?" You surrender jealousy at the feet of His Majesty with a prayer: "Take this, Lord. All my emotions I offer at your feet. I am thine, and all is thine."

Practiced daily, any one of these spiritual therapies will free you from jealousy and bring harmony into your life.

Judgment:
The Mind's Disease

Charlotte came to my workshop on "Human Relationships and the Dynamics of Spirituality." She told us that she was in her mid-forties, and that it was only in the last year that she seemed to age, and her hair had turned prematurely gray. Her daughter, she said, was her problem.

"For five years, I have meditated, but now my daughter has robbed me of inner peace. I want the best for her, but she goes for the worst. I was paying for her education, but she dropped out of college to buy a new car, the worst thing she could have done. Now her future will suffer. Recently, she started going out with someone who is her inferior. Only bad can come from that. All this turmoil has affected my health and my meditation. Is there something I can do to change her, to make her see the light, so that I can get back my peace?"

D. Yes. You can help yourself. Right understanding is your highest priority. To want to help others is natural, especially your children. But once they come of age, the most you can do for them is to point the way. You can tell them what you would do under the same circumstances and tell them the possible outcome of their choices. Then we need to leave the rest to God, to trust and let go. Eastern spirituality teaches that God is absolute Truth, nameless and formless existence, and that the same Truth has taken the form of the entire universe and everything in it. When we try to run his show, we get hurt, and so do others.

To set ourselves up as constant judges of what is good and bad about people and things and events simply means that the Force behind the helm is still invisible to us. This tale from the East puts it clearly.

Once there was a poor Indian villager who owned nothing but a white horse. Richer neighbors came to his hut one day and said, "You are so poor! Why not sell your horse?" "No," he said. "I don't want to." The next day his only horse ran away. "How unfortunate you are!" cried the neighbors. "Your only possession of value is gone. How unfortunate!" The wise man said, "I don't know whether I am unfortunate. All I know is that my only horse ran away."

The next day, the horse came galloping back leading a pack of twenty-one wild horses. Neighbors flocked to his door. "How fortunate you are!" they exclaimed. "You own twenty-two horses. Oh, how fortunate!" "I don't know whether I am fortunate," said the villager. "All I know is that I now have twenty-two horses."

Next day, the villager's only son got on one of the wild horses. The horse galloped away and threw the boy with a thud. His ribs were broken and villagers brought him back to the hut totally incapacitated. Again, the neighbors visited. "Oh, how unfortunate!" they exclaimed. "Your only son is totally incapacitated." "I don't know whether I am unfortunate," said the villager. "All I know is that my only son is incapacitated."

Next day, an army captain knocked on every door

in the village. "We're at war," he declared. "Every man between the ages of sixteen and sixty is conscripted." The only man who did not go off to war was the villager's son.

The redundancy of judgment is the point of the story. Not only is it a waste of time; it is harmful.

Learn to relax. Then learn to meditate properly to deepen your inner contact with God. Surrender is born of that contact and inner peace is born of surrender. You may profit from reading and meditating on *The Way* by Seng-ts'an, third Zen patriarch: "The Great Way is not difficult for those who have no preferences. When love and hate are both absent, everything becomes clear and undisguised. Make the smallest distinction...and heaven and earth are set apart. If you wish to see the truth, then hold no opinions for or against anything. To set up what you like against what you dislike is the disease of the mind."

If you work towards the goal as Seng-ts'an describes it, not only will your life change, but so will everybody around you.

Somebody once said that body and soul are God's gift to humankind, and mind is society's disease.

Knocks and Knots:
Seek the Giver, Not the Gifts

Ben had drunk heavily for fifteen years. The habit had cost him his family, his business and his home. Since joining Alcoholics Anonymous two years ago, he has experienced a spiritual conversion. Now he lives a spiritual life and works on the fourth Alcoholics Anonymous Step: taking a fearless moral inventory of himself. Still, he has difficulty reconciling his ongoing suffering with his inner transformation.

"I see other peoples' lives running smoothly," Ben said. "Mine is full of knocks and knots. I get out of one jam, and another one is waiting even before I do anything. I believe in a Higher Power. That Power picked me up out of the gutter. Thanks to that Power, I'm still dry. But why should all the problems continue just as they did before my conversion?"

D. When you shut off a fan, the blades continue to turn from the force of momentum. The same momentum operates when you quit an addiction. But our problems do not lie in what is happening out there. The real problem lies in our preconceived unrealistic expectations. We see things we call "good" as coming from our Higher Power. Those that give us pain we think must come from a lower power. The truth is that there is one Power only, not two.

Consider this story: A saintly old monk was walking down to a river near his monastery. A madman came from behind, knocked him down, and ran off with his water tumbler. The monk lay prostrate on the ground. A few minutes later, one of his brothers found him. "Who did this shocking thing to you?" he cried. The old monk barely got the words out. "The Lord," he whispered. While the brother ran for medical help, a villager came along carrying fresh milk. Seeing the monk in pain and unable to move, he poured some milk into a cup and raised it to the old monk's lips. Then he too ran for help, leaving the cup there. When the brother came back with a healer and saw the monk, he asked, "Who gave you this milk?" The old monk whispered, "The same Lord who knocked me down."

This oneness of vision is what we have to cultivate. Some of Joel Goldsmith's books can guide you in this: *The Infinite Way; Parenthesis in Eternity;* and *Practicing the Presence.* The most helpful of all spiritual practices for attaining this oneness of vision is redirecting your inner attention. Shift it from the "gifts" of pleasure and pain, and focus on the Giver instead.

Mental Noise:
Empty Your Cup

Theresa sold insurance. Divorced and thirty-two, she led an active social life and met with community action and discussion groups several times a week. Every morning for an hour, she did yoga postures and breathing exercises. "They keep me young," she said. A year ago she and her friend Penny spent three weeks in India visiting a God-realized sage.

"When we sat in his presence, my friend left her physical consciousness and went into a trance. Afterwards, she told me that repeated waves of ectasy filled her body and that she felt electric-like movements up her spine. When Penny came out of it, her face looked superhuman, like the face of a madonna.

"My experience was the opposite. I came with questions that the sage answered, but I felt nothing special, and I wondered why."

D. Not everybody responds in the same way to a spiritual master. Some masters draw us; others don't.

T. I know that, but somehow I felt that the problem was my lack of preparedness. When I asked him why I did not feel what Penny felt, he said, "Your friend's cup was empty. Yours was full. It had no room for anything new." I still don't understand what he meant by that.

D. What were you thinking of as you sat there?

T. Of him. I wondered how enlightened he was, if there was anything going on between him and the young women around him, and what I should be feeling.

D. That is a full cup. Expectations, judgments, preconceived ideas of how a sage should act and what you should feel in his presence.

T. How can anyone avoid that?

D. Through spiritual practice. That is what it is for. When you observe your mind, you become aware that it is the source of all your problems. The more you stand back and witness it, the quieter your mind becomes. Seekers in the East are enjoined to approach masters with an empty cup, which means to come in silence, sit in silence, and leave in silence. That means keeping the body still and the mind free of the kind of static that filled yours as you sat there. No preconceived ideas. No expectations. No judgments. Few or no questions.

T. How will my questions be answered if I don't ask them?

D. Masters "see" your questions as they arise in your mind. If your mind is quiet, you "hear" their answers instantaneously.

T. What is wrong with asking questions out loud?

D. Nothing is wrong. Verbal questions have their place, but the power of silent transmission is mightier than words. Electric current in India operates at 220 volts. Our appliances run on 110. Like a transformer that brings the voltage down to where we can make use of it, the mind pulls higher knowledge down to its own level. Mind is not our highest faculty. If we depend upon mind to understand everything, we lose a lot.

T. Is this idea peculiar to the Vedic tradition?

D. Not at all. Throughout the book *The Imitation of Christ* which I always carry with me, you find the same message repeated in different ways: "I teach without the noise of words."

T. Penny and I want to go to India next year to visit the sage again. How can I prepare myself?

D. Meditation is the best preparation. If we do not meditate, then the silence at the back of our mind gets absorbed by the mental chatter.

T. Penny told me how she meditates. I tried it but I got nowhere. Now I am discouraged.

D. Be patient and trust, and you will find a way. Lawrence LeShan's little book *How to Meditate* will give you all the help you need to start. Penny's method may not be the right one for you. Choose a method that you feel comfortable with.

T. One of the reasons for my busy mind is my involvement in so many discussion groups.

D. A spiritual practice that could help you in those groups is receptive listening. First, determine before certain meetings that you will input nothing verbally, or at least as little as is feasible. When you feel the urge to speak, don't express or suppress it. Observe the urge as coming not from you but from a force outside of yourself, from the active forces of nature that surround and interpenetrate you. Just draw back your consciousness, and watch the impulse to speak until it dissolves. It *will* dissolve.

Second, determine beforehand to ask no questions. When questions arise in your mind, stand back, look at them, and ask yourself mentally, "To whom did this question occur? Who is perceiving this question?"

T. What does that do?

D. That acts on the unruly, restless mind like a leash on a puppy. Instead of identifying with the mechanical flow of haphazard thoughts, you return to your natural state as witness Consciousness. As the witness, you have mastery over your mind; your mind no longer masters you.

T. What if my question is important and it really has to be answered?

D. Ask it as a last resort. Before you ask, see if you can perceive the answer *behind* the flow of others' words.

The third and last step is to practice listening to others with your heart instead of your mind. Listen in mental silence to what they are saying so that the message behind their words goes into your heart without getting distorted by a busy mind.

In these ways, you can spiritualize your life and empty your cup. When you see the master again, your cup will be ready for him to fill.

Muchness:
A Modern Pathology

Nadine wrote articles and gave workshops on journalism throughout the United States. She came to my workshop on "Creative Problem-Solving" because of a problem she called "muchness."

"It's like a disease," she told us. "Before I give a lecture or write, I prepare for it with every book I can find on the subject. Sometimes I have fifty to a hundred books on my desk, most of them saying the same thing." Nadine said that the "disease" manifested in many ways in her life. Three-quarters of the clothes that hung in her closet she did not wear. Yet she couldn't throw them out. "When I cook a meal for myself there's enough food for three people. I eat more than I should, but I still have to throw away a lot. Is there a spiritual approach to this problem?"

D. Muchness as a value clutters many lives. Our culture prescribes it. Television, radio, the press, billboards, shopping malls, and conventional education tell us over and over again that "more is better." More possessions, more wealth, more distraction, more activity, more food. Muchness cuts deep grooves in our minds. "Much" means success—"little" means failure. Muchness is a device born of contemporary society to

58

give us a false sense of security. Having much does not minimize the risk of insecurity. Risks come from everywhere, and they come all the time. Security lies in strengthening our tolerance for insecurity. Insecurity is the nature of life. Most of us know this at heart. If we did not, we would not seek spiritual experience, nor would you be here.

It seems to me that the way to cope with this "disease" is the way we cope with any transformation. What you want is a different value by which to live, a value that makes more sense in your heart than the one that has governed your life thus far. Next, you want to transform your habits of body and mind to correspond with it. I would call this value "the law of absolute necessity."

Here is how you can do it. For years you have meditated unconsciously on muchness. Change your meditation. Meditate consciously instead of unconsciously, and switch the object of your meditation from muchness to absolute necessity. A good way to begin is by reflecting on this law as it applies to your profession. I am sure you know *The Elements of Style*, the classic on how to write by Strunk and White. Strunk wrote that a sentence should contain no unnecessary words, a paragraph no unnecessary sentences, for the same reason that a drawing should have no unnecessary lines and a machine no unnecessary parts.

I heard a well-known writer say that he never uses a reference book for his first drafts. He writes "from the inside out." Before he touches the typewriter, he sits in his meditation room and asks his higher self, "What is it that needs to be said?" Not until he receives complete guidance does he get up. By doing that he finds the germ of his message first, and adds the hay later. Using so many reference books to begin with, you are piling up the hay first, and trying to find the germ within it. That is the outside-in approach where muchness is the law. This is like going from store to store to find out if they have anything you need, instead of deciding what you need first and going to buy it. You want the inside-out approach, which is always governed by the law of absolute necessity.

Let's apply this law to food. Every spiritual tradition stresses the need to waste nothing, to cook and eat only enough for the body's requirements to perform its work. More than that becomes toxic because the body cannot handle it. Spiritually speaking, too much food relegates the act of eating to sensual pleasure rather than to survival.

The key to making the law of absolute necessity an integral part of your life right now lies in the Biblical axiom: As you believe, so shall it be. Picture yourself and believe yourself already living by the law, living it in your kitchen, your clothes closet, your study, in sleep, and in speech. Meditate on the law with a silent mind every morning, before retiring, and as often as you can throughout the day. In the East, it is said that whatever you do for forty days in a row becomes a habit. Give the exercise forty days of your life. When the new law becomes habit, you will discover a spiritual truth. Muchness distracts, destroys, and gets you hooked on quantity. The law of absolute necessity keeps your priorities right and gets you hooked on quality.

The law of absolute necessity reminds me of a framed poem I saw on the wall of a doughnut shop in New York City:

> As you ramble on through life, brother,
> Whatever be your goal,
> Keep your eye upon the doughnut,
> And not upon the hole.

60

Negative Emotions:
Repress, Express, or Release?

Life changed for Allison on her fifteenth wedding anniversary when her husband walked out and never came back. Bitter anger drove her from one psychotherapist to another. The more she talked about what happened, the angrier she got. Soon, her inner anger colored her thoughts throughout the day. When her latest laboratory test showed malignant tissue, her doctor advised her to quit psychotherapy and focus on positive thoughts instead. Allison did not know how.

"For eight years, I heard that expression was healthy," she said. "Express everything you feel, my therapists told me. So I did. I'd go home, shut the window, and scream. Then I'd take Jack's clothes and fling them against the wall with every four-letter word in the book. Whatever I found that belonged to him I'd rip, break, tear, or smear. After those sessions I felt spent, used up. I had no idea how much damage that did to my body until my sickness came to light. Expression got me into this mess, but repression is even worse. Now I don't know what to do."

D. Literature is replete with the effects on body, mind, and spirit of expressing and repressing negative emotions. Books such as Hans Selye's *The Stress of Life* and Norman Cousins's *Anatomy of an Illness* present lucid explanations of how negative emotions damage body processes. *Ayurveda*, an ancient science of healing indigenous to India, teaches that repressed anger alters the flora of the small intestine and the gall bladder. In *Ayurveda, The Science of Self-Healing: A Practical Guide*, Dr. Vasant Lad writes that anger causes inflamed patches on the mucous membranes of the stomach.

Spiritual teachers from all traditions, past and present, know the dangers of expressed and repressed anger. In the *Summa Theologica*, St. Thomas Aquinas wrote that expressing anger brings a rush of blood, tensing of muscles, and acceleration of the heartbeat. "Such physical disturbances impede our power of reason." *The Philokalia*, a compilation of writings of the early Desert Fathers, states that an angry man, even if he were to raise the dead, is not acceptable to God. Sage Swami Sivananda said, "Through anger, a man loses all spiritual merit in an instant." "Rascal sage" Gurdjieff made a similar remark: "The expression of anger can at once explode all the substances prepared in the spiritual laboratory and leave a man inwardly empty for a long time." The Buddhist scripture, the *Dhammapada*, says that anger is like a chariot careening wildly and that only he who curbs it is a true charioteer.

A. But if I just think of positive thoughts like my doctor told me, what am I supposed to do with my negative emotions?

D. The mature, healthy way to handle negative emotions is neither expression nor repression but release. Gurdjieff said that the process of release frees us immediately of negativity, and it brings into play a faculty that thrusts us forward on the spiritual path.

A. How do I do it?

D. Let's say that the thought of Jack arises in your mind. Instantly you feel bitter. Instead of pursuing the thought and surrendering to bitterness, shift your inner posture. Stop focusing on Jack. Focus instead on the bitterness that arose in your mind. Let only the bitterness remain as the object of your inner attention. As you observe it, you will become aware that the bitterness is not you; it is separate from you. It comes from outside yourself. When you stand back from it, observing it and refusing to identify with it, you will see it subside as suddenly as it arose. In the beginning of your practice, the bitterness may surface frequently. But the more often you refuse to identify with it, the less often it will occur.

A. When the anger dissolves, am I back to the mental state I was in before it came up?

D. You are further ahead. You are more conscious because you have separated yourself from your emotions. Sri Aurobindo offers a discipline that follows the process of standing back and observing anger. He suggests that as soon as you observe what is going on in your lower nature and separate yourself from it, call for the descent of divine light and peace into that part of yourself to transform it. Eventually that Force will replace all mechanical and negative movements with its own light.

The practice of not identifying with negative emotions, and opening inwardly to the descent of the divine Force will transform your entire nature, improve your health, and turn your life around.

Pride:
In the Spirit of Vedanta

Pete and his wife recently joined a Vedanta society in a midwestern city. They meditated together and were trying to spiritualize all aspects of their lives. Pete was a graduate student of comparative religion and served his university as a committee coordinator. He had just written his first book.

"Ego is my root problem," Pete said. "I try not to feed it, but it jumps back at me. Finishing my book took three years. When I finished it, my wife and close friends said that it was a fine piece of work and that I had a right to be proud. Pride boosts ego, I told myself, and I don't want to go that route. My wife says that honest pride is not egoistic."

D. "Honest pride" is a contradiction in terms. How can pride be honest?

P. Why not?

D. Pride implies an independent agency of action. Who is the agent?

P. Pete.

D. According to your Vedantic studies, what is this thing called "Pete"?

P. In my understanding of Vedanta, Pete has an ever-changing body and mind. Pete's body consists of the five great elements. The subtle body interpenetrating it which contains the mind consists of the five elements in their subtle state. The elements are products of the three *gunas* or primary cosmic qualities: inertia, activity, and equilibrium. The gunas emerge from the cosmic energy of Brahman, the Impersonal Reality—the nameless and formless existence.

D. Then where is Pete?

P. I don't know. He just vanished!

D. What is it that just vanished?

P. Pete's mental projection that Pete is an independent agent of action. When I reflect on it that way, it is easy for me to see that there is no separate entity called Pete. But when I'm caught up in the flow of life, Pete comes back!

D. That is because we meditate on Truth for one hour a day and for the remaining twenty-three hours, we fuel illusion.

P. Lately, I have tried to bring my meditation into my life. Often, when I stop for a few moments and witness my body and mind in action, I see Pete as pure energy, the dance of energy. Brahman is the Dancer, and I am his dance. Is it correct to think in this way, to think of oneself in terms of a conglomerate of energy?

D. According to Vedanta, it is correct to consider Pete as the energy, the dance, the action of God. Once I heard an American Vedantin say that he thought of his body-mind complex like an ad hoc committee of hormones.

P. Yet I sense something in me that is permanent and static.

D. That something is the Consciousness that witnessed Pete when Pete was a foot long, that witnesses Pete now that he is six feet long.

P. Then who wrote the book that has drawn such praise and has Pete's name on it?

D. The book was written by the Universal Mind. It

was not written by an individual agent of action for an individual purpose. In *I Am That*, Sri Nisargadatta says that the Universal Mind does everything. "It makes and unmakes everything, and the Supreme imparts reality to whatever comes into being." He described the Supreme as immense peace and boundless love.

P. Let's get back to my book and my pride. What can I do at the moment that pride rears its head? What statement can I grasp that will give me instant light?

D. A profound statement in the form of a question might help you. It comes from a chapter in Thomas á Kempis's *Imitation of Christ* called "The Secret Judgments of God—That We Be Not Puffed Up With Our Own Good Works." It asks, "Shall the clay glory against Him that formed it?"

P. Does Vedanta have a similar statement or question, something I could hold on to to counter the pride of an author?

D. How did you do your first draft? By computer, typewriter, or pen?

P. I alway draft with a pen.

D. In that case, I will share a statement of profound insight that a Vedantic master in India made to a Yugoslavian writer. Like you, the writer had just finished a book, a translation into his language of a massive spiritual encyclopedia. His fellow academics commented that the work was superb. The writer asked whether he was justified in taking any credit. The master's reply to him is my reply to you: "When you finished writing the book," said the master, "did it ever occur to you to thank the pen that wrote it?"

Problems:
In the Spirit of Zen

Elliot had spent five years working for the U.S. State Department in Japan. Recently, he was transferred to a "primitive" area in North Africa where he found conditions too hard to cope with. On leave for a few weeks, he was pulling every string to get out of his present post. In Japan, he had learned Zen meditation, but he did not know that life is a zendo, a field for practicing Zen.

"Conditions are impossible," Elliot said. "When it's 100 degrees in the shade, the electricity goes off. Not a fan budges, let alone the air conditioner. I get into a shower and all I get is hot water. A minute later, all I get is cold water. Half the time I need the phone, it does not work. Worst of all is the fact that I can't meditate with the insects and the heat. For three months I haven't sat. I heard that if I didn't meditate for forty days I'd lose whatever progress I've made. True?"

D. Possibly, but that is not the issue. The issue here is that Zen never leaves meditation on the coat hook of a zendo. Zen means freedom from reaction, balance of mind, nonidentification with sensations, likes, dislikes, cravings, aversions, illusions, and preferences. Zen is the art of living, not the art of living well.

Somebody asked the Buddha what real welfare means. The Buddha said, "Balance of mind in spite of all kinds of vicissitudes—victory, defeat, profit, loss, honor, or shame—with a smile."

Any Tom, Dick, or Harry can get along fine when life runs smoothly. Near-perfect circumstances provide no tests, no challenges, no soil for inner growth. Gene Tunney, the world champion fighter, said that he got to be world champion only by pitting his strength against resistance. Your post provides a rare frictional massage for a Westerner.

Biographies of all the great sages are replete with self-imposed austerities. To rise above the protests of body and mind, Swami Sivananda got into the icy Ganges at 3:00 A.M. every day and stood in the water up to his neck repeating a mantra. Who among us Westerners can practice austerities like that? Our latitude of tolerance is low, but that is not our fault. Push-button high-tech lives deprive us of the chance to use the muscles of tolerance that Third World people have. This is one reason why they are generally much more relaxed than we are. The higher the latitude of tolerance, the lower the tension.

To progress on any spiritual path, we need to trust and surrender to the wisdom of the Universal Intelligence that put us where we are. All placement is purposeful. Try to rise above your mental protests. Accept your post as a challenge instead of a hardship, and start meditating again. In the true spirit of Zen, focus not on the provocations but on your reactions to them. Then you will see them for what they are. At the end of your sitting, you might repeat mentally the following axiom and contemplate its inner meaning. This will give you inner peace independent of your external world.

"The worth of a man lies not in what he has but in what he can do without."

Relationships:
From Discord to Accord

Sisters Debbie and Clara came to my workshop on "Human Relationships and Spiritual Healing." They belonged to an active Catholic order, lived in a small inner-city retreat house, and worked together to rehabilitate refugees from the East.

"We help others," Sister Debbie said, "but we can't help ourselves." She told us how they fight about trivia from the moment they get up. "About everything— stupid things like whose turn it is to wash the dishes and linens, who gets the heel of the bread loaf, who should do the grocery shopping."

"Our fights have become addictive," Sister Clara said. "We asked our Bishop for permission to go our own ways, but he told us that a difficult relationship is the best way to grow in the spiritual life. If it is, we've failed. The only thing we have agreed on in a long time was to come here tonight."

D. An elderly Methodist gentleman shared with me a simple and powerful healing exercise that could help you. You need not sit together to do it. Try it out in the privacy of your rooms every morning and evening.

Stand and stretch your limbs. Then sit in a comfortable chair with your back straight. Roll your neck around slowly to reduce its tension, and stretch all your facial muscles. Slow down your breath, and make your exhalations as long as you can. Sense that you are exhaling all your tension and inhaling peace. After some minutes, picture a triangle. The apex points up, and the apex is the Cosmic Heart—Jesus or love. At the bottom left is angle C, Sister Clara; angle D at the right is Sister Debbie. Love, the apex, functions through Spirit. The Holy Spirit is the line that connects C and D, L and C, L and D.

Refine the picture in your mind as sharply as you can. Keep observing it on the screen of your consciousness at the inner center of vision between your eyebrows. If thoughts intrude, don't identify with them. Let them pass like strangers who knock at your door and then walk away. Above all, do not think of one another or of anything that has transpired between you.

When the picture becomes very clear, transfer your consciousness to the spiritual heart at the center of your chest, just under the rib cage. Focus on an opening there and on this prayer: "Lord Jesus, let the love of Spirit flow between us." Then open yourself to the flow of it—slowly, from D to C, C to L, L to D; D to L, L to C, C to D. Over and over again. Feel the movement of the Holy Spirit running between the two of you, fuelled by love at the apex. Twenty minutes at each sitting is all you need for a total change in your relationship.

C. It sounds so simple, yet I sense its power. Why should something so simple be effective when all our efforts have failed?

D. Probably because your efforts were made on a level of mental consciousness. This exercise takes you out of that level. It opens your heart directly to the power and love of God. That is what transforms. Unless we are hospitable to a power functioning on a plane higher than our minds all our efforts yield only cosmetic changes. We can talk about Jesus for the rest of our lives, but words and thoughts do nothing. Change must occur in our consciousness.

Another reason your efforts may have failed is that you concentrated on one another instead of on God. That is a common habit. You focused on the area of discord instead of the area of accord. Constant thought of any problem fuels its magnitude and intensifies its impact on us. Yet most of us do that most of the time. One can almost say that most people are unconsciously addicted to bringing their problems to perfection instead of perfecting a solution.

Self-Transformation:
The Free and Easy
Way to Change

Isabel came to my workshop on "Self-Transformation: Secrets of the Mystics." The tension and demands of her job as a day and night waitress had driven her to seek peace in meditation. But many years of careless living habits made it difficult for her to get up early enough to meditate regularly.

"My trouble is discipline," she told us. "I don't have it, especially when it comes to sleeping and eating. I go to behavior modification workshops, but nothing changes. I came here to find out what I can do to get some discipline into my life."

D. St. Teresa of Avila should have been a psychiatrist. Somebody once asked her a similar question, and she said, "If you want to acquire any virtue, imagine you have it, and you are halfway there."

Self-image plays the inner tune. Behavior dances to it. For a long time, you have repeated, "I have no discipline. I have no discipline." So when your alarm goes off at 5:00 A.M., your subconscious mind plays its only relevant record: "No discipline. No discipline. No discipline." That record is like a pattern that a tailor uses to cut out a suit. As is the pattern, so is the suit. When the record plays, the mind activates the hand to shut off the alarm, and the body, to go back to sleep. In *Psychocybernetics*, Dr. Maxwell Maltz explains this phenomenon succinctly: "Behavior can never be inconsistent with self-image."

Please study *The Power of Affirmation*, a short publication written by spiritual master Subramuniya, published by the Himalayan Academy in Hawaii. He teaches us how to break out of one mental force field and enter into another. "If one feels, 'I can't,' he cannot. He has to reverse this pattern and *change the flow of magnetic mental force,* enliven its intensity by saying orally and feeling through all the pores of his body, 'I can. I will.' " The master suggests repeating this a hundred times a day to reprogram old patterns of thought.

Let's apply these principles to specific habits of sleeping and eating. First, change your general mantra from "I have no discipline" to "I have discipline. I am disciplined." Repeat this as often as possible to offset the influence of your previous mantra. Second, when your mind is receptive to suggestion—for example, before you fall asleep—visualize the *mental equivalent of* the action that you want. To get up early, picture yourself getting out of bed every morning at 5:00 A.M. and meditating for an hour. Do this as often as you can.

Let's look at eating habits. If you see yourself as a person who eats anything at any time, then of course you *will* eat anything at any time. To change that habit, alter your picture of yourself to the mental equivalent of the person you want to be. Visualize yourself as a disciplined eater, eating when and what you plan to eat, and no more. Picture yourself weighing what you want to, wearing what you want to, living as you want to live. The law of the mental equivalent is the key to changing habits, acquiring virtues, and transforming your life.

I. I would think that most peoples' minds would continually revert to old habits, and those old records have much more power than the new ones. How do you combat this problem?

D. In *The Mental Equivalent*, Emmet Fox offers three keys to surmount this resistance: CCI—Clarity, Constancy, Intensity. Clarity means getting your goal clear in your mind. Constancy means feeding your new self-image with supportive thought at every possible moment. When the old record begins to play through mechanical habit, replace it instantly with the opposite image. Intensity means fueling your new image with deep feeling. It should never be just a mental idea for you; your heart and every cell in your body should feel it. As master Subramuniya put it, "Feel it through all the pores of your body."

The Bible says, "As you believe, so shall it be." It does not say that as you wish, so shall it be. Wishing is vague, weak, wishy-washy. Believing is power. Believing has power. Believing makes things happen.

There is a Sanskrit mantra called "the eternal secret": *Mana eva manushyānām kāranam bandhamokshayoh.* What the mind is, so is man.

Sex-Mastery:
Why and How

Before Gregg got a job as a truck driver, he had taught arithmetic in a rural school. As a teacher, he had little money and time. Driving a truck gave him both. Behind the wheel all day, he had ample time to think about Reality, and he could meditate without disturbance in his truck just as he did in his apartment. He came to my workshop on "Self-Mastery: Keys from the East" to learn how to reconcile spiritual and sexual drives.

Gregg told us about his guru. "She is American," he said, "a grandmother who lives in California and has reached the zenith of human potential. No matter what happens, she is always blissful. She radiates peace, love, and light.

"The last time I was out there, she talked about sex. Unless we master the sex urge, she said, our spiritual progress is limited. She didn't explain why. That statement has bothered me since. I love the peace I get in meditation. I want to go deeper, really deep. But at the same time, I'm a normal guy with normal urges. I have women friends in different towns. When you're free the way I am, it's hard to ignore the urge. What do you think my guru meant when she said that? And how can I reconcile my two opposing urges?''

D. Sex energy contains a mystical force that few people know about. When its inherent power is not expended outwardly, it gets transmuted into ojas, the substance required to attain Cosmic Consciousness. Ojas yields vigor, power, and magnetism not only to reach high states of being but to succeed in every field, especially creative work.

Let's say you have one hundred dollars in your account. You plan to spend some of that on a correspondence course that could open the door to a new career. You are not sure how much the course will cost, but you don't want to think about it today. Tomorrow is your birthday, and the party you are hosting is uppermost on your mind.

At the supermarket, you buy hors d'oeuvres, cheese, sweets, wine, beer, and champagne. The tab comes as a shock: $95.00! That leaves only $5.00 for your course. This balance of five dollars is what your guru referred to. Sex energy acts like a bank account. What is in the account can go in only two directions, out or up.

G. My problem is that I have a very sexual nature.

D. That is not a problem! It is a gift. A highly sexed nature is a sign of spiritual force. Many of the greatest spiritual and creative men and women had highly sexed natures. Transmuted sex power is an elevator that can lift us to Cosmic Consciousness and creative genius.

G. I can understand the idea of transmutation. But is there anything else wrong with expressing the sex urge as it comes up?

D. The renowned Buddhist master Sri Goenka says that ''free'' sex relations are harmful and that they throw people off their mental balance. He said that people who have come to him who have played "the game of free sex" are unbalanced.

G. What is the connection between imbalance and free sex?

D. Perhaps it lies in what I heard a well-known macrobiotics teacher say. He said that every time we have sexual intercourse with anyone, we take into ourselves not only our partner's sexual energy but also his or her level of consciousness. Promiscuity means that we are imbibing many different and possibly conflicting levels of consciousness.

G. How do you master the sex urge?

D. With three "arithmetical" processes: substitution, subtraction, and addition.

Let us look at substitution. Let's say you are driving your truck through a town where an attractive girlfriend lives. You picture her in your mind, and almost instantly, sexual desire manifests itself. Sri Goenka says that expression and repression are both harmful. He says that at the moment you sense passion in yourself, you should observe the sensation rising in your body. As you observe it, the passion will lose its power over you.

Sri Aurobindo teaches that as the sex urge rises, you see it for what it is: a movement of the lower nature. You do not struggle with it because if you do, it will win. Instead of struggling, you draw back from the movement. Detach yourself from it, observing it as something that is not you. The forces of nature outside of us impose themselves upon us. We need not fight their imposition anymore than we need to open our door to every knock and argue with strangers out there.

So the idea is to refuse consent to the imposition and not to fight or yield to it. Stand back as the Witness

Consciousness. It is quite astonishing how fast the impulse dissolves. When it does, that sexual energy within us becomes transmuted into a powerful force to use for other goals.

G. What about subtraction?

D. To master any behavior, we must know what causes it and then subtract the causes. The Vedas speak of three gunas or qualities that govern man's life on earth: *tamas, rajas,* and *sattwa.* They are not really qualities; they are the stuff of which the universe consists, like strands of a rope that constitute the rope. We can actually say that all there is in the universe are these three modes of existence. Tamas is the quality of inertia, darkness or ignorance; rajas is activity or restlessness; sattwa is equilibrium, light, and balance. Sri Aurobindo describes these gunas as passivity, passion, and poise.

When tamas prevails in the body, we feel tired and sluggish and we want to sleep. When rajas prevails, we feel active, restless, or passionate. Foods governed by tamas such as stale foods, meat, fowl, fish, and eggs increase the heaviness of the lower body and make us more conscious of its urges. Rajasic foods such as garlic, onions, and hot foods, trigger sexual desire. Spiritual masters advise meditators to abstain from all these foods. To experience the silence, to sit motionless and open oneself to light, one needs to eat sattwic foods that channel higher energy, foods such as grains, vegetables, dairy products and fruit.

G. Does only the Vedic tradition teach this?

D. All mystical traditions teach that the food we eat plays a major role in sex-enslavement. In *The Philokalia,* a compilation of writings by the early Christian Fathers of the Desert, St. Neilos writes that sexual desire is more closely related to what we eat. He says that the proximity of the belly to the sexual organs is itself a testimony to the intimate connection between food and sex. Christian saints, he writes, fled towns to avoid corrupt company and kept themselves alive on nuts and berries and whatever grew on trees and shrubs. He quotes Mark I:6: "John, too, dwelt in the wilderness of Jordan eating locusts and wild honey." St. Neilos concludes that we should satisfy our bodily needs with very little effort. St. Maximos says that the demon of unchastity is powerful and attacks violently those who are lax about matters of diet.

G. Do Christians still observe these suggestions?

D. Contemplatives do. Orders such as the Trappists follow the rule of St. Benedict and adhere to simple vegetarian diets. When St. Benedict was asked, "What food shall we Christians not eat?" he replied, "If the food you want would run away from you on the table, don't eat it."

G. And Buddhists?

D. In Buddhist monasteries that I have visited in Nepal, Burma, and in the United States, I have seen only vegetarian food. Sri Goenka says that flesh foods and spicy foods agitate the mind, and that if we take meditation seriously we should not eat them.

So far we have looked only at the stimuli of taste, but if we are sincere, we will apply subtraction to stimuli that provoke our eyes, ears, nose, and skin. This means avoiding television shows, novels, songs with suggestive lyrics, pictures that stimulate thoughts of sex, and the proximity to people who trigger the sex urge in us.

The third process, addition, refers to practices like Hatha Yoga, Pranayama, meditation, repetition of mantras, and acquisition of virtues to purify the heart and mind.

G. I can appreciate the need for those practices because I know what meditation and yoga have done for me. I like the idea of a witnessing response to the sexual urge and I see the reason for vegetarian food. But those other subtractions! Subtracting eye and ear and nose and skin stimuli—that's a tall order for a man!

D. Man is a tall creature. Look at a moth. A moth is so attracted to light that it cannot stay away. The light burns it and the moth dies through the lure of sight. Because fish can't resist worms, they perish through the hook in bait, only through the sense of taste. The smell of certain flowers attracts a bee so much that it forgets the passage of time. Dusk comes, the petals close, and the bee gets caught—through its sense of smell. Deer hunters in the East hire bamboo flutists to hypnotize deer. The deer rush to the music and land in the hunter's net, perishing through the sense of sound. Elephant hunters dig a big hole in the ground and put an artificial she-elephant on top of it. The male gets so excited by the thought of touching her that he rushes over and falls into the hole. The lure of touch brings an elephant to ruin. These creatures perish through only one sense organ. Look at the plight of human beings. We've got all five senses working at the same time!

Sex-mastery seems tough but you have the requisite for spiritual success. You want to "go deeper," and your wish is sincere. Sincerity is the key to self-mastery. That key will operate on your next birthday when the thought of a party comes up. Instead of rushing off to the supermarket, you will consider your priorities first. Then you might ask yourself, "What will it be this time? Champagne or the course?"

Suffering:
From Resistance to Challenge

Divorced after twenty years of marriage, Laura lived alone in a city apartment. She worked as a buyer in a department store and spent her free time trying to meditate and reading spiritual books. Depressed by her inability to meditate, she sought help at the workshop. What Laura did not grasp was the essence of the spiritual process: the movement from individual to Universal, the submergence of the individual will into the Universal Will.

"This summer my mother came to live in my town," she told us. "Now she is in a nursing home near me. Earlier, she had lived with my brother and his family, but when they left the country, she came here. Her demands on my energy and time make me bitter and resentful. The worst part of it is that she interferes with my spiritual life. I find the situation intolerable, but I don't know what to do about it."

D. Let us look at the matter objectively. The situation of a mother living in a nursing home near her daughter is not uncommon. Many aging parents live even under the same roof as their offspring, a situation that demands much more energy and time. Your response of anger at what you consider to be an imposition on your life is a response *not* to the situation but to your own resistance.

The facts that your mother is near you, and that she needs you, and that she has no one else to care for her now imply that the situation also answers some need in your life at this time. The need may not be apparent; still, it exists.

Alter your angle of vision. Instead of regarding the situation as intolerable, view it as a challenge. Use it to mirror your current inner state. See in that mirror the underlying cause of your resistance, and work on it. If no such opportunity had arisen to work on yourself, you would not have seen that area of resistance, and very probably, you would undergo similar suffering in the future. To get beyond any circumstance, we have to go through it.

The Buddha said that all suffering comes from resistance. Instead of repeating to yourself, "This is a pain in the neck," repeat, "This is a golden opportunity. I will use it for three purposes: (1) to take a deeper look at myself and clean out the psychological cobwebs, (2) to reciprocate the care that my mother gave me when she might have preferred to do other things, and (3) to clear away all negative feelings in our relationship so that when she leaves her body she takes with her no resentment towards me and leaves me with no guilt to harbor for the rest of my life."

Resist not, say the sages, and all suffering will cease.

Suffering:
In the Spirit of
Christian Mysticism

Sister Mary attended my workshop on "Suffering: Perspectives from East and West." She taught at a Catholic school in Pennsylvania where the constant suffering of a younger, humble, and devout sister troubled her. Unable to accept the law of karma, she sought the meaning of suffering within the Christian orientation. "Carrying a cross is what Christian life is all about," she said. "But what I can't get through my head is why the best of us seem to suffer the most."

D. Christian mystical literature is replete with stories that point to why. Here is a tale from the life of St. Teresa of Avila that makes a relevant point.

Teresa was setting up convents throughout Spain for the glory of God. One night, she was riding her horse from one village to another. A heavy downpour soaked through her clothes and body. Strong winds shook her balance. At one point, while she crossed a wobbly, narrow bridge, the bridge collapsed. Down into the river she went, horse and all. Miserable and sick, she swam to the riverbank, looked up, and said, "Lord Jesus! How can you do this to me?"

The Lord's voice answered, "You are never given what you cannot bear, Teresa."

"But why do this to *me*, Lord? Me, your faithful servant?"

"That is the way I always treat my friends," said the Lord.

Teresa, who was on familiar terms with her Lord, puckered her lips and said, "You see, Lord? That is precisely why you've got so few!"

2
The Dynamics of
Spiritual Growth

Choosing a Path: Easy Guidelines

Twenty-three-year-old Kevin was confused. "I've hung out with many spiritual groups," he told us, "and read many books from all traditions. But I still don't know where I belong. I am looking for the right path."

D. To find a path you have to know why you are looking for it. Why do you want a path?

K. I want a proven way to work on myself. I know that there is a lot more to life than food, sleep, and sex. Right now I feel mechanical.

D. Moving from mechanical reaction to conscious action is the chief aim of the Gurdjieff Work, and one of the aims of all spiritual practices.

K. How do I find the best path?

D. Paths don't compete like cars. We each select a path that suits our nature. Perhaps it is more correct to say that before we choose a path, a path has chosen us.

K. How?

D. Inherent in each of us is a nature that is predominantly devotional, logical, or intuitive. In the East one often hears this question: If you love "sugar" (God or absolute Truth) would you like to *taste* it or *become* it? The desire to *taste* sweetness is the desire to love and worship the Lord as other than oneself. This inner pull points to the path of devotion or Bhakti Yoga. On this path, one surrenders to the personal God—to Jesus, Krishna, Shiva, Ram, Buddha, Allah, the Divine Mother, or to any divine ideal.

Wanting to *become* sugar indicates an inherent pull toward putting an end to one's ignorance through knowledge of the Self. This inner pull points to the path of knowledge, Jnana Yoga.

A third powerful path to realization is the king's yoga, Raja Yoga, with its eight practices for liberation. Raja Yoga attracts seekers with logical minds. What makes the difference in paths is the vehicle stressed in practice. In devotion or Bhakti Yoga, the heart is purified; in Raja Yoga, the mind; in Jnana Yoga, the discriminative or intuitive faculty.

K. Where does Buddhism fit in?

D. Once I read the insightful statement that Buddhism climbs the ladder backwards. It negates appearance. It explores all phenomena—forms, sense objects, sense organs, body, mind, feelings, sensations—until the seeker perceives that form is totally nonsubstantial. In this sense it is like Vedanta or Jnana Yoga.

K. What is the difference between them?

D. While many Buddhists see no ultimate Self behind the apparent emptiness, Vedanta states that even to perceive the fact that form is nonsubstantial requires Consciousness. Subtract Consciousness from anything, writes Sri Swami Krishnananda, and you find nothing, for nothing can exist without it. The Self—Consciousness, existence, and bliss—is the heart and center of all things. To experience this heart is the goal of Jnana Yoga.

K. Does Vedanta or Jnana Yoga involve any devotion?

D. Every goal involves devotion. A Bhakta yogi is

devoted to the personal Supreme. A Jnani is devoted to Brahman, the impersonal Self—Atma Bhakti, it is called. A Buddhist is devoted to the goal of freedom from the illusion that forms are real. Tibetan Buddhists are devoted to gods and goddesses whom they worship to imbibe their qualities—compassion, love, wisdom, courage, harmony, peace.

K. I am still not sure how to choose my path.

D. Once I wrote a questionnaire to help people select a path. Perhaps a few of the questions might help you. Has jealousy ever troubled you?

K. Many times, and I hated to feel it in myself.

D. What did you do to get rid of it?

K. Talked to myself. "This is childish," I would say. "You can't change people. All you can do is to change yourself."

D. Would the jealousy go away?

K. Not immediately, but I would think of other things, of my achievements for example, or of people who respect me.

D. Can you give us an example of how you deal with fear?

K. Once I camped out in a Montana forest. Some wild animals were prowling around at night. I was scared. I kept saying, "Calm down, Kevin. Relax and you'll be all right." Eventually the fear went away.

D. It sounds as though you would feel at ease with the path of Raja Yoga. Devotional persons might have said, "Lord, protect me. Remove my fear and replace it with your love and peace." They might repeat over and over: "Though I walk through the valley of the shadow of death, I will fear no evil, for thou art with me. Thy rod and thy staff, they comfort me."

Intuitively or intellectually inclined seekers on the path of Jnana Yoga would not identify with fear. "I am not this emotion," they would repeat. "I am the all-pervading luminous Self.'' The Jnani would stand back and observe the fear as not his own.

D. How would he look at the bear?

D. A Jnani sees that the nameless, formless existence and Truth has taken the form of the entire universe and everything in it. So he or she would think, ''That bear is a form of my Self.'' This inner attitude tends to dissolve aggression in other creatures—humans and animals.

K. How would a Raja yogi react?

D. Raja yogis know that all words have a corresponding emotion. Not wanting to harbor fear, they would change their thought to the opposite: ''Om Courage. Om Courage.'' Those words evoke a corresponding inner attitude that allows one to cope intelligently with the situation.

You can find step-by-step instructions for all these paths, their stages of development, signs of progress, and how to surmount the obstacles en route in texts written by Eastern spiritual masters.

K. If my long-distance goal is Self-realization—like my ten-mile run—what are my immediate goals, my one and two-mile runs?

D. Constant remembrance of Self or God, cultivation of virtues, and spiritualization of your life.

K. I know the prize I would get for winning a ten-mile run, but I am not clear about the reward for the ten-mile spiritual run.

D. The ultimate reward for all these practices is the same. Initially they appear to be different, and they are expressed in the vocabulary of their tradition. In Bhakti Yoga, the reward is union with God. In Buddhism, it is the pure Buddha mind which has pierced all illusion. In Jnana Yoga, it is release from the bondage of ignorance, from thinking that you are a body subject to birth, decay, and death, to knowing you are cosmic, limitless and infinite—the Source that empowers you and everybody else to run the ten miles.

A common prayer repeated in Indian before meals can help us to understand this prize:

Om Brahmaarpanam, Brahma havi, Brahmaagnau Brahmana hutam. Brahmaiva tena gandavyam, Brahma karma samaadhina. (The food is Brahman, the eater is Brahman, the process of eating is also Brahman.)

Similarly, the runner, the ground, and the process of running—all this is the Self.

The grandest prize of all, then, is the perception that the Self has become subject *and* object, and that nothing exists but Self alone.

Discrimination:
Discriminate, Don't Judge

Barbara, a confident court reporter, had a problem reconciling her need to distinguish "right" from "wrong" with the injunction, "Judge not." "Time and again we spiritual seekers hear that we are to harbor no opinions, no value judgments, no preferences," she said. "But if we did, then anything would be just as good as anything else or just as bad. We would have no basis for decisions."

D. For this reason, discrimination is the most important qualification for a seeker. Here is a story that explains the point.

A monk was walking down a village road in India. He was repeating, "Everything is God. Everything is God." Ahead of him, he saw an elephant lumbering along at a slow steady pace with its tamer at its side. When the elephant saw the monk, she picked up her pace. The tamer yelled, "Quick! Quick! Get off the road! The elephant will kill you!" But the monk paid no heed. He went on chanting, "Everything is God. The elephant is God." Within seconds, the elephant was upon him. She wrapped her trunk around the monk's body and hurled him into the air. Down came the monk to the side of the road, where he lay with all his ribs broken. The tamer ran up to him and yelled, "Fool! Fool! Why didn't you run the other way when I warned you?" The monk barely whispered the words, "Because everything is God. The elephant is also God." "Sure," said the tamer. "But so am I!"

Discrimination is an essential requisite, especially on the path of knowledge where the seeker practices perceiving the One *in* all and *as* all. Attitudes like "this is good," "that is bad," "she is no good," and "he is ok" are harmful value judgments that the mind makes. Discrimination, on the other hand, is a product of the higher, intuitive faculty. Discrimination enables us to choose the friends, the actions, and the environments that help us to reach our goals and to drop those that steer us from them. Between "good-bad" and "appropriate-inappropriate" lies a world of difference.

God:
A Yardstick to Gauge
Our Nearness

Bernard, a retired engineer who meditated regularly, followed the Christian mystical tradition. More than anything else, he told us, he wanted union with God before he died. "How do I know whether I'm getting close?" he asked. "Is there a yardstick by which a man can gauge his closeness to God?"

D. Once, I heard a young American student ask the same question of an Indian sage. The student was one of fifty Westerners sitting cross-legged on the floor of a terrace in a Himalayan ashram. The master sat on a high-backed chair in front. "Excellent question," he remarked. "Yes, indeed, there is such a yardstick. But first, I want to ask you a question. How many desires do you have?"

"What kinds of desires?" asked the American.

"Any kind," said the master. "For example, do you want a good home? Would you like to marry? Do you want to heal the knee injury you got playing football? What about your career? Do you want a good job, more money, specialized education? When you get a home, will you want a swimming pool?" To almost every question the young man nodded.

"Now I would like all of you to get out your pens

and notebooks," the master said. "Make a list of every desire you think you have. And number them." The Westerners wrote line after line, page after page. Ten minutes later, the master looked at the young student. "Young man," he said, "how many items do you have on your list?"

"Twenty-three," the American answered.

"Fine." He looked at a middle-aged woman. "And you?"

"Eighteen," she said. He pointed to a twenty-year-old girl. "How about you?" he asked. The girl blushed. "Fifty-five!"

"Fine," said the master. "Now take an imaginary ruler and measure the length of your list." He watched as the Westerners made their mental calculations. When they had finished, he looked back at the young man. "Now you have your yardstick," he said.

"I don't understand," said the American.

"You see," the master explained, "the length of your list of desires is the measure of your distance from God."

God:
Perceiving Him in the World

Clinton lectured in English at a prestigious east coast university. He told us that he thought of himself as either a Catholic Hindu or a Hindu Catholic. "I'm not sure which one it is," he said. "I love the Mass, and I go every Sunday. But Vedanta fills my heart and my mind and my bookshelves. To reconcile both disciplines is not easy, but I'm not aiming for that. At this point, I want only understanding.

"Vedanta and mystical Christianity urge us to perceive the Lord through all names and forms. What is the method? How do you perceive Reality in the world? Suppose I want to practice this right now with you. What do I do first?"

D. Presuming you are wearing your Christian hat, let's follow the advice of *The Philokalia*, a compilation of writings by the early Fathers of the Desert. The fathers tell spiritual seekers not to limit their perception of visible things to what their senses observe. They tell us to search with our intellects for the Essence that lies within all creatures.

What you do first is to withdraw your consciousness from your sense of sight. Your eyes will still see Darshani in front of them. But your consciousness will not identify itself with your eyes. Instead, you will use your intellect or discriminative faculty to recall that eyes are inert. They are matter. What you are really cognizing is not a pair of eyes but the Light, Intelligence, and Consciousness that animates them, the Light and Intelligence of God. You are cognizing pure Consciousness in this form called Darshani.

Next thing you try to realize is *who* is cognizing. Surely, it cannot be your eyes or your intellect. With some surprise, you realize that the cognizer in you is the same cognizer that you perceive in me. What is happening here is not an interaction between Clinton and Darshani. It is Consciousness perceiving itself in its objectified forms. Constant reflection on this truth can bring you to the goal very quickly.

C. Yet there is an essential difference in the way Vedanta and Christianity perceive God in the world. Can you clarify the difference?

D. Creation is central to Christian doctrine. In the Christian ethos, the essence of God is the core of our being. Yet we are separate entities, independent agents of action. Thus, Christian seekers practice perceiving God *in* all names and forms.

Manifestation, rather than creation, is central to Vedanta. According to Indian philosophy, the entire universe is a manifestation of God or Spiritual Consciousness. So followers of Vedanta practice perceiving God *as* all names and forms.

The difference, then, between the Christian and Vedantic perception of God in the world boils down to "in" versus "as." What a perfect question for an English professor! The preposition makes the difference.

Grace:
The Price Is Hospitality

Forty years old and divorced, Harry lived alone in a
low-income efficiency apartment. For a decade, he had
battled a drinking problem. Unable to look it squarely
in the face, he never joined Alcoholics Anonymous.
Some months ago, the problem got worse.

"I was out walking with a friend of mine," he said.
"We were on our way to lunch. Weeks had passed
since either of us had taken a drink. When we passed
a bar, Joe nudged me. 'Man!' he said. 'Would I love
a Manhattan!' Instantly, the thought of it possessed
me. My mind's eye saw the red liquid and the cherry.
My mouth tasted its sweetness. My stomach felt it
coursing along its lining. Intense desire filled me.
Within minutes, Harry and I were sitting on a bar stool
and downing our third Manhattan.

"That night we landed in the hospital. After a week,
we got out, and again we walked together to a cafeteria.
Suddenly, Harry grabbed my arm. 'What do you say?'
he asked me. 'How about one—just one—only one—
cocktail?'

"Minutes later, we were drinking again, nonstop.
Again, we landed in the same hospital. I told this story
to a minister friend of mine. He said, 'You must ask

Jesus for his grace the instant your friend nudges you. You have to ask for grace to get it.' The problem is that the moment I see or even hear the word 'cocktail' or 'Manhattan' I can't resist. How do you get grace when you can't resist?''

D. Many years ago, I played a lot of chess. As you may know, chess is a battle between two armies. Pawns are the little guys, the soldiers who fight the battle on the front lines. One of the first things you learn is how to protect them. In olden days, soldiers wore suits of armor. Nobody could attack them from the front or the back because their armor was impenetrable. Only at their sides were they vulnerable. For this reason, the only way an opponent can attack and capture a pawn on the chessboard is from an adjacent position. So your first job as a chess player is to learn how to avoid placing your soldiers in a position of adjacent vulnerability.

Let's apply this principle to you. You are walking down the street alone or with a friend. Of course, a real friend would never pull you down. Let's say you are walking alone. Store windows attract you. Your head turns to the right: In a bakery window is an appetizing strawberry shortcake. In the sports store next to it, you see a jogging outfit. Next to that—uh oh!—brown colored bottles of liquid that make your life a hell. Instantly, you turn your back to them. Instead of visualizing a Manhattan or a swig of whiskey, you visualize these words: "I have had enough hell! Grace! Here I come!" and you bolt off like hell in the other direction. The *desire* to bolt off is your task. Grace does the rest.

Like the sun, grace never discriminates. The sun never says, "I will shine on Joe but not on Alan." If we sit in a dark room with shaded windows, how can we get sunlight? We have to get out and walk into it. To save your pawn, you get it out of the enemy's line of attack. To get grace, you have to walk out of nongrace.

We must become hospitable to change. If we do not, then just as today is like yesterday, every tomorrow will be like today. The price tag for what you want is hospitality. Pay it, and all the grace in the universe is yours.

Guru:
To Have or Not to Have

Mark studied music theory and clarinet at college. Since his freshman year when he went to a meditation workshop given by a visiting Indian monk, he had meditated regularly. He had also practiced meditative superlearning techniques as taught by Dr. George Lozanov. In recent months, a wave of spiritual experiences had come through his meditation. He asked about these and then about the controversial matter of a guru. ''Is a guru really necessary?''

D. Why do you have a clarinet teacher? Why can't you just study clarinet from a book?

M. I can learn some things from a book but not everything. A book can't tell me if my mouth position is correct, if my tone is round enough, or how to phrase a cadenza. For that I need a teacher. But isn't my clarinet one thing and my spiritual life another?

D. To learn anything—clarinet, violin, word processing, German, computer programming, maths, portrait painting, mechanics, or carpentry—we need a teacher. A teacher is somebody who has attained mastery in the field, walked the route, reached the goal, found the shortcuts, and figured a way out of the inevitable jams. On the spiritual path, the ground we tread is far subtler and stranger than a clarinet, a violin, a computer, or a car. We are trying to rise from one dimension of consciousness to another. We need help to see where we are going, how we can get there, and how to get out of our own way. That is the function of a guru. The word means "giver of light" or "remover of darkness."

M. I do not have a guru. Yet I meditate and live on the path of Light. Isn't that due to the guru within?

D. Somebody had to start you off. Who taught you why and how to meditate?

M. The visiting Indian monk.

D. He was your first guru, the messenger of your inner Self. He came to you when you were ready, and he woke you up. When somebody asked Sri Nisargadatta if a guru is inevitable, he said, "It is like asking if a mother is inevitable. . . . It is the inner guru [the Sadguru] who takes you to the outer guru as a mother takes her child to a teacher."

M. Will another guru come along?

D. If and when you need one. The Sadguru within attracts what you need.

M. Some teachers say that we have only one guru throughout our life.

D. As far as they are concerned, they may be right. My personal experience runs contrary to that. I have studied and practiced under the guidance of several illumined masters. One woke me up. Others contributed different dimensions to my development. I am grateful to all of them.

M. Is it important to hang out with a guru?

D. Some say it is. Others say it is not. In the Indian tradition, living near a saint or sage is generally considered to be vital for liberation. Sri Nisargadatta qualifies this. "Living near" does not mean breathing the same air. It means trusting and obeying, not letting

102

the good intentions of the teacher go to waste. Have your guru always in your heart and remember his instructions—this is real abidance with the true. Physical proximity is least important. Make your entire life an expression of your faith and love for your teacher—this is real dwelling with the Guru.

Papa Ramdas, the Indian-born sage, said that we cannot progress much when we stay with a guru for a long time because we get attached to the form instead of the Formless. Another problem is that we tend to take the proximity to a guru as a substitute for spiritual practice. No matter how great a guru is, he or she can never do our practices for us. We have to carry the ball ourselves.

M. If a guru does show up again in my life, how will I recognize him or her? I've heard that a lot of quacks call themselves gurus.

D. Sages say that seekers have a right to test gurus. Observe them carefully before you accept them, and ask yourself: "Is the teacher open? Does he or she encourage disciples to visit other great masters? Has he conquered lust, anger, greed, hatred, jealousy, ego, and fear? Is he looking for name and fame?" More important than what he does, however, is what or where he *is*. A real guru should not be just virtuous. He should have gone beyond body and mind, space and time, beyond all duality. Only then will his words become imperishable seeds in our lives.

M. How can I judge this?

D. Ask yourself: "How do I feel when I am in his presence? What does he bring out in me? Am I growing inwardly?" Sri Nisargadatta said that if you turn into gold through the proximity to your guru, then you know that you've touched the philosopher's stone.

M. I was told that you have to surrender to the guru if you want to make progress.

D. Why have a guru if we don't surrender? Surrender to the outer guru is actually surrender to the inner. Since many of us can't do that by ourselves, we need an external guru to break down the resistance of our ego, and overcome restlessness and inertia. Eventually we learn that life itself is the supreme guru. Every person who crosses our path—every creature, event, success, failure, pleasure, pain, frustration, anxiety, love, hate, sight, and sound—come to us as a lesson. They come not through chaos but by design. The less we surrender and accept the lessons of life, the more we need an external guru. The greater our acceptance, trust, and surrender to life, the less is our need for the outer guru.

Indian sage Papa Ramdas said, ''One ought to depend upon the inner promptings alone for one's right guidance in life.''

Ultimately we realize that behind all teachers, and behind the moving Hand of Life lies the supreme, silent Sadguru—the formless, indivisible, all-pervading light of Self.

Let Go and Let God:
Put Your Baggage Down

When Marty left a low pressure job in computer programming to set up an independent software company and got his first government contract, life changed overnight.

"Before, there was time for everything," he told us, "time for my work, time for my wife and kids, time to relax. Now there's no time for anything. Nine to five, six, even ten doesn't do it. Sometimes I work till midnight to meet deadlines. Last week for two nights in a row, I slept in my office to save commuting time. My blood pressure is way up, and my doctor told me to 'let go.' I came to this workshop ('Let Go and Let God') to find out how—not the 'let God' part because I'm not much of a believer. 'Letting go' is all I want. My problem is that I'm chasing a tail that's running faster than I am."

D. Can you place yourself mentally on a train? You're going on a long journey, and you've got a good seat. Up front is a very capable conductor. But there's a problem. Because of poor habits or wrong understanding, you did not put your luggage down. You are balancing a large suitcase on your head. On your lap, you are holding another one. A third one you are carrying in your arms. What do you think of that picture?

M. Ridiculous.

D. What should the traveler do?

M. Set his baggage down, of course.

D. Why?

M. It's being carried by the train anyway. He doesn't need to hold it.

D. Precisely. For that reason, you can let go.

M. I don't know what you mean.

D. Put your baggage down. The train of life is carrying it.

M. What's my baggage?

D. What thoughts are filling your mind right now?

M. The face of a government official when I have to tell him his program isn't ready. Other demands I can't meet. Contracts I want to get, but I still don't have a foot in the door. Personnel who sometimes work, sometimes don't, who are competent at times and fools at other times. College fees for my daughter, a car for my son, an addition to the house.

D. That's the baggage you have to put down.

M. A train is one thing; its got a conductor. But who's the conductor in my work? I am. I'm conducting the train of my work, work that comes out of my office. I'm responsible for every bit of it.

D. As the scripture *The Bhagavad Gita* puts it, you are entitled to the action but never the fruit.

M. What's the difference? The fruit should be the natural outcome of an action.

D. Should it? How can it be? The results of your efforts depend on infinitely more than how many hours you sit in front of your computer. Let's start from the beginning.

Your qualitative output depends on, among other things, the degree of light to which you are open as

106

you program. The absence of impedances, such as tension, is crucial. The finer and freer your thoughts, and the more relaxed you are, the finer and higher the forces you can channel.

The physical and mental states of your staff matter, too. Do they work under an external compulsion to turn out quantity or through an inner desire to please? The mood of the official who evaluates their work also matters. So does the official's motivation, which may be colored by a conflict of interest. For these and countless other reasons, we cannot control results nor make things happen. We can only do our best and surrender the rest.

M. What you are saying is that everything happens by chance.

D. No, not at all. Nothing happens by chance. A Universal Intelligence that never sleeps and never takes a vacation is working behind and in and through every scene of our lives. It creates, sustains, and dissolves for purposes that are not individual. That Intelligent Power spins out universes and arranges the intricate network of life, the exchange of vital forces between humans and plants, the cyclical appearance and disappearance of suns and moons, summers and winters, days and nights.

M. But I'm a person who has to see a thing in order to believe that it exists.

D. How much of what your lungs and your kidneys and your liver are doing now can you see? None. Yet the work is going on, and you take it for granted. You have no control over the autonomic processes going on in what you call your own body. They are happening without your consent and without your knowledge.

Just as we have billions of cells in our body, each of us is a microcosmic cell in the universal macrocosmic body. Your brains, hands, input, and output do not exist for you alone but for the entire macrocosmic network. When we exaggerate our self-importance, we get out of tune with that Reality. How interesting it is: We know we do not control our entry into the world and we don't control our exit. Yet somehow we think we control the middle part.

M. I'm ashamed, maybe for the first time. When you said "the middle part," it struck me that here I am, almost forty-five years old, and I've never stood in awe of anything in my life.

D. How fortunate you are that you realized that at forty-five. Many people never do.

Here is my suggestion. There are many good yoga schools in your city. Sign up for a class for adult beginners.

M. I go to a gym whenever I get the chance.

D. But what you need is relaxation, and yoga will give you that. You needn't believe my words; just experience it for yourself. From the very first session you will learn how to relax your body and mind.

At home when you are relaxed, look at the commitments you have undertaken. Whatever you and your staff can do well between the hours of nine and five, keep. Relinquish the rest. Tailor your needs and desires accordingly. Schedule time after five and on weekends for yoga and for leisure activity that fulfills you rather than distractions like TV, and save time for your family. Most important, when you get up and just before you retire, sit in a quiet place in your home for some minutes to meditate. Your yoga teacher will show you how. At that time, when you still the mind and stir the heart, channels of higher energy open up. As a result, you can turn out more and better work in less time. And, blood pressure drops.

Through daily Hatha Yoga and meditation, you will

let go of the thought that Marty is running the show. A daily reading from the *Bhagavad Gita* can also help you. Through it you will grasp the dynamics behind the axiom, ''We human beings are entitled to the action, but not to the fruit.''

Love:
The Myth of "I Love You"

Pamela never married. Now in her fifties, she wanted a relationship, but rarely did she meet single men. A nun in the Catholic school where Pamela taught advised her to contemplate on Jesus instead. Pam could not see how that would bring her the bliss she yearned for.

"Years ago, I fell in love often," she said. "That state of being in love, that one state of mind, changed my whole personality. It made my life worthwhile, even just to say and to mean, 'I love you.' Of course, that happened when I was younger. Nobody asks me out these days. Do you think that even a little of the joy of a relationship could come from contemplation?"

D. You've got the situation reversed. The fact is that worldly joy is a mere shadowy reflection of the bliss of contemplation. Let's take an objective look at this state called "bliss," but first, let's clarify contemplation. In the Christian mystical sense, the sense referred to in your tradition, contemplation means what meditation means to the East: the science and art of stilling the mind.

Suppose you're on a ship in the middle of the Pacific Ocean. The time is midnight. It's a lovely summer

110

night cooled by soft breezes. The moon is full. All alone, you walk out on deck. No one is around. Before your eyes lies an infinite expanse of sea. Waves crested with the jeweled reflections of a golden moon rise and subside everywhere around you. For a moment, you stop breathing. Extraordinary peace and bliss fill your whole being.

Where did that bliss come from? From the scene or from you?

P. From me.

D. Precisely. It came from you, not from the scene.

P. But it took the scene to bring the bliss out of me.

D. Now you've hit the secret. That particular scene had the capacity to *arrest your thoughts* for a split second. In that instant in which your thoughts were arrested, you experienced the tip of the tip of the iceberg that is the bliss of your Self, your true Self, the formless substratum Reality. That is what happens when your thoughts stop. If you analyze your moments of joy, whether they are evoked physically or mentally, you will see that the joy of them comes from within you, sparked by the capacity of a person or thing to arrest your thoughts even for a split second.

In contemplation, thoughts cease for much longer than an instant. The bliss you experience then is so much deeper and more real and so infusing that it makes the joys of the world appear like child's play. Worldly joys are pale reflections of the inner bliss from which they come.

When you love somebody, you are loving the bliss of Self, the Self within you. Love doesn't come from the man you are with. If it did, you would have the same feeling whenever you were with him. That never happens because both he and you live in a state of constant change. Change is an unwritten law of life.

Your nun friend is right. The joys of contemplation

111

will transform your personality. If you visit a Trappist or Benedictine order, one of the brothers could give you instructions. Books like *The Cloud of Unknowing*, and Brother Lawrence's superb classic, *The Practice of the Presence of God*, will guide you and inspire you.

If your mind begins to doubt the power of contemplation, recall these three facts: First, contemplation means stilling the mind. Second, when the mind is still, you experience bliss. Third, getting bliss firsthand frees you from depending on external stimuli to release it from within you. If this is too much to remember, recall this simple equation: The words "I love you" really mean, "When I'm with you, I love me."

Love Your Enemy:
From Theory to Practice

For thirty-five years, Cathy worked as a legal secretary. Due to retire, she planned to spend leisure time in biblical studies and church work. Cathy came to my workshop called "Human Relationships and the Spiritual Way" to learn how she could reconcile the faults of "sinners" ("when I know they are wrong") with the Christian precept "love your enemy."

"I'm a Christian," she began. "I live it every day of my life. But the one injunction to love our enemies has always struck me as impractical for our day and age. Look at the world around us. Violence, drugs, and corruption are everywhere. How can you love people who live like that? I think the teaching applied to a period of time that was different from ours. Do you agree that now it is impractical and impossible?"

D. No. I don't agree. Not only is it possible today; it is imperative for our survival.

The path of life has two roads. One is secular; the other is spiritual. The secular road is ego-centered; the spiritual one is Christ-centered. You have to decide which road to take.

C. I have made my decision. Long ago, in fact.

D. Let's see. Let's take a look at your friends. Who are they?

C. God-fearing Christians, good people who live by the Commandments.

D. Good. What do you get out of their friendship?

C. A lot of support. They give me solace and comfort when things go wrong, and they prop me up when I'm down. They're pillars to lean on, shoulders to cry on.

D. Now I'm going to ask you to stand back from Cathy. Take an objective look at what Cathy just said. When someone deflates her ego, her friends prop it up again. Correct?

C. Yes.

D. Do you see, then, that the people Cathy calls friends are those who support her ego-structure?

C. Sure. What's wrong with that?

D. Nothing at all if you are not on the spiritual path. Everything is wrong with it if you are. What stands between us and God? Between our present state of consciousness and Christ-Consciousness? Ego.

Listen to these words from the *Imitation of Christ* in a chapter called "Peace is not to be placed in men": "Thou oughtest to be so dead towards persons beloved as to wish, as far as thou art concerned, to be altogether without any human fellowship. So much the nearer doth man approach to God as he withdraweth himself the farther from all earthly consolation." Earthly consolation thickens the crust of our ego. The fatter our ego, the greater our distance from God.

Let's take a look at Cathy's so-called enemies. Who are they?

C. Women and men who lie about me. To my face, they're sweet. Behind my back, they run me down. People who have cheated me, disrespected me, and even humiliated me in front of others.

D. Okay. Now tell us this: do you believe that the Lord is omnipresent?

C. Of course.

D. What does that mean to you?

C. That he is everywhere.

D. Is he also in the people who vilify you?

C. Sure. He must be. But they don't know it. That's the problem. They don't recognize him.

D. That's *their* problem, not yours. They will carry their garbage to their graves. You don't need to cart their garbage to yours.

C. I don't know what you mean.

D. Christ said that when someone slaps your cheek, you should turn the other one too. He did not say, "When someone slaps your cheek, go get your friends to pat it."

Christian literature makes the point clear: When people vilify, cheat, slap, humiliate, frustrate, and lie about us, our task as true Christians is not to observe the law of tooth for tooth and eye for eye.

C. But I don't do anything to them in return.

D. Yes, you do. Harboring negative feelings towards people is an action. Calling someone an enemy is an action. Returning hate for hate, in heart and mind, is an action. Resisting evil is not the Christ-centered path. It is the way of the ego.

C. What should a Christian do?

D. Sit quietly and send them a gust of loving wishes for their peace, good health, and long life.

C. But how will that change them?

D. Changing them isn't our homework. Changing ourselves is. But what a surprise! When we return good for evil, evil changes.

C. But, to love people who are disrespectful, who cheat, lie, hate, rape—that is asking the impossible.

D. Then Christianity is impossible. Any Tom, Dick, and Harry can love people who are good, honest, and easy to get along with. That is not the Christian challenge.

Some years ago, I went to a large discount shop in

New York with an elderly Methodist gentleman. The store was busy, and the salesgirl who waited on us was very rude. Her disrespect and impertinence irritated me, and I wanted to report her. My friend smiled at her and restrained me. Later that day, I asked him what his goal in life was. His answer shamed me: "To be a channel of healing and love for all those who hurt me." John is a true Christian.

C. How did he reach that state?

D. Through steady practices in self-transformation.

C. I would like to try a few simple disciplines, especially to cultivate real Christian love.

D. The key to transformation lies in the Bible. "Love your neighbor as yourself." Loving your Self is prior to loving a neighbor. We cannot put on a garment of love and make it work. Love is a noun, not a verb. Love is what we are, not what we do.

C. What does it really mean "to love yourself?"

D. Your Self is the ground and core of your being—God. It is your spiritual heart, and love is its nature. It is in you—yet it is more correct to say that you are in it. It is your center and the center of everything in the universe from an atom to the solar system.

C. Why isn't it more apparent?

D. When dross covers a light bulb in your bedroom lamp, your room will be dim. Remove the dross and you have light.

C. How do I get to that point?

D. Through the process of purifying your body, mind, and heart. I will share with you seven simple practices that can help. First you can purify your body through postures given in books on Christian yoga. Second, you can purify your mind with the powerful Jesus mantra that brought so many Christians to spiritual perfection: "Lord Jesus Christ, have mercy on me." You will get all the guidance you need for this

116

practice from *The Way of a Pilgrim*, a little book written in the nineteenth century by an unknown Russian seeker (published by Image Books). This spiritual guide shows how the Jesus mantra brought the pilgrim to enlightenment.

C. What gives the mantra so much power?

D. A mantra is the sound body of God. As you call the name, you deepen your inner contact with the state of consciousness that it represents. Also, our minds tend to wander like drunken monkeys. This restlessness prevents the light of God from shining through us. A mantra puts a check on that. It keeps our minds focused on God. You can say that a mantra acts like a spiritual subway strap.

Third, read the lives of Christian saints for inspiration, especially St. Thérèse of Lisieux. Before the end of her short life, Therese said that the harsh treatment by her superior did much for her spiritual progress. The reason is that our acceptance of pain, mental and physical, brings us to much higher levels of consciousness than pleasure ever can.

Fourth, whenever you see your mind resenting or hating, try to catch it in the act and look at it as though it were a third person. You might say to yourself, ''There goes Cathy again. Like a pendulum, her mind is swinging nonstop between the fear of pain and the desire for pleasure. But 'I'—the Self—am beyond both pleasure and pain, beyond the pendulum, and beyond Cathy.''

Fifth, when you see or think of your so-called friends or enemies, mentally superimpose the face of Jesus on theirs. Try to perceive Jesus smiling or frowning at you, praising or rebuking, inflating or deflating your ego. That steady practice will take the edge off your value judgments.

Sixth, for a few minutes every morning and even-

117

ing, sit quietly in a comfortable chair. Reflect deeply on one line from the prayer of St. Francis: "Where there is hatred, Lord, let me sow love."

C. How will this help me?

D. What you meditate on, you become. This happens because the mind, which is subtle matter, actually takes the form of the object that it concentrates on. When it thinks of God or love, it becomes very fine and subtle because God and love are formless.

Last, consider the fact that you cannot press into permanence anything, not a state of health or an attitude of mind—yours or anybody else's. A friend today can be an enemy tomorrow; an enemy today can be your friend tomorrow. To become a true Christian, one should not use the terms "friend" or "enemy." The truth is that no one is either.

Mantra:
"I Am He"—Or Am I?

Sixty-year-old Stella designed textiles and spent her spare time reading spiritual books. She came to my workshop called "Who Am I?"

"Recently, I saw a well-known actress on television playing a spiritual role and repeating the mantra, 'I am He.' Since then, I've been repeating it too. I have always believed that God is in me and not only outside of me. Will this mantra bring me to enlightenment?"

D. What do you mean by the "I am"?

S. Everything. My personality, character, body, mind, habits, ambitions, concerns—all of it.

D. Then the mantra probably won't help you. The mantra does not mean that Stella is God. Stella is not God. God is appearing as the "I AM-ness" of Stella. If you could understand that you are the silent Reality beyond the changing body and mind, the mantra would be fine. Because you do not have this perspective, other mantras would do you more good.

S. But I have heard it said that everything is He, changeless and changing.

D. True, but we cannot jump to the top of the ladder. We have to climb it rung by rung. On the path

119

of knowledge, we start out by negating the unreal, negating all changing phenomena through the practice of *neti neti* (not this, not that). From there we get to a rung where we see that we are pure awareness, the perceiver who perceives changing phenomena. On the next rung we realize that we are not an individual viewing the phenomena of our body and mind: we are the cosmic noumenon looking at its cosmic phenomena, the static Self looking at its dynamic form. Only on that top rung do we perceive that we are the all.

Sri Nisargadatta writes: "If you can remain anchored in the immaculate identity between the noumenon and the phenomena, which is your total potential, there cannot exist any basis for the imaginary bondage from which you want to be released. Your notion of bondage is just the illusion that you are an autonomous entity, subject to temporality and the Karma cause-effects."

When you say that you feel you are your personality, body, mind, habits, and so on, then obviously, you take yourself to be a limited, changing individual form. To transform this perspective, you need a mantra that will help to purify the sheaths around the Self—physical, pranic, mental, and intellectual. Once the sheaths are purified, the Self will shine through them without impedance. Then you may not need a mantra to remind yourself you are That.

S. But you have to start somewhere.

D. True. But starting with "I am He" when you consider yourself to be body, personality, and mind, is pointless and counterproductive. The right starting point for that mantra is the understanding that you are not your personality, body, and mind.

S. Then other people are also doing the wrong thing by chanting it?

D. Nobody can answer that. If their starting point

is right, they may be doing what is appropriate for them.

S. What is the difference between the "I" of "I am hungry" and the "I" of "I am He"?

D. When we say, "I am hungry, I am cold, I am lustful, I am scared," we identify our essence with the sensations of our body and the desires of our mind. To put this in a nutshell, the identified "I" is our obstacle. The unidentified "I AM" is our goal.

Meditation:
Love Your Object

Nate and Joan came to my workshop on "Meditation:
What, Why, When, Where, and How." Due for retirement after forty years of electrical repair work, Nate
wanted to spend his leisure time understanding himself
and life. Joan wanted to learn more about Buddhism.
A small statue of the meditating Buddha that a friend
brought back from Nepal triggered her interest. She
unscrewed the bottom part and found a tiny piece of
folded paper "like you see in a fortune cookie,"she
said. On it was a Buddhist mantra transliterated into
English. "As soon as I started to repeat it, my depres-
sion fell away. Recently I began to meditate on the
statue itself."

"I don't like her doing that," Nate said. "That's idol
worship and it makes me uncomfortable."

D. Are your parents living?
N. No.
D. Do you keep pictures or other remembrances of
them around the house?
N. Pictures of them are all over the place. We have
a sculptured bust of my dad, too.
D. Why do you keep it around?

122

N. It reminds me of them, and I like that. They were great people—intelligent, kind, loving. Nothing is wrong in remembering them.

D. Nor is anything wrong in remembering the Buddha, his infinite wisdom, compassion, and love.

N. But why does she have to meditate on a statue?

D. The mind needs a hook on which to hang its thoughts. Nobody can sit down and "think of God." God is too vast, too all-embracing. Besides, the mind cannot know God. Finite can not know infinity. Meditators find an object that represents the qualities of God that they love and want to imbibe, and they concentrate on it to the exclusion of all else. When the concentration reaches a level of absorption, their consciousness pierces the object. Essence touches essence and merges into itself. That hook is vital. Often I picture the object of concentration like the middle point of an hourglass. At the bottom, thoughts are diverse; they run everywhere. When the rays of consciousness focus on the middle point, they lead the meditator up and out to the formless Reality.

N. I want to meditate too, but not on a statue. What method can I use?

D. What do you love?

N. I love working with electricity.

D. The aim of meditation is to experience Reality. What is the highest reality of your work?

N. Electricity itself.

D. What does it look like?

N. It never shows itself. But you sure can feel it, and you can't live without it.

D. Is there anything in the human being that you cannot see but you sure can feel, and you sure can't live without?

N. Spirit, maybe, but I don't know what that is.

D. Transcendent Spirit is pure awareness. Self-luminous, formless, boundless, and indivisible, it is beyond space, time and causation. Like electricity that is hidden in a wire, this hidden being is your reality. In your work and in life, the real is unseen.

N. Where does my body come in?

D. Where an electric wire comes in. What is the function of wires?

N. To channel electricity.

D. Body and mind are channels of Reality.

N. If consciousness is indivisible, it means that there is only one of it. Is that right?

D. Right.

N. Then why are we all so different?

D. Electricity is one. Yet there are enormous differences between a fan and a heater, a toaster and a refrigerator. The function of an appliance determines its appearance. Each of us not only performs a function of the Divine; we *are* that function.

N. Could I arrive at an understanding of who I am through meditating on electricity?

D. I heard a spiritual master say that we should meditate only on what we understand and love. You have worked with electricity all your life. You understand it and love it. Use it as a hook to hang your mind on.

N. If Joan meditates on the Buddha and I meditate on electricity, what is the difference in where we end up?

D. No difference. Enlightenment is the aim of all meditation. Let electricity be your inner guru. Follow it to its Source, and let the Buddha lead your wife to Source. The word *budh* from which the name "Buddha" is derived means "to wake up." As the world around the Buddha slept and dreamt on that full-moon

124

night in May many centuries ago, the master sat under the Bo tree until his mind pierced the bubble of illusion and he awoke. The Buddha continues to wake up his devotees and to illumine their way to wisdom, bliss, and common sense.

Meditation:
What and How

Since she opened her New York psychotherapy practice, Gail has felt that the conventional approach misses the point. "It doesn't reach the whole person," she said. Even after incorporating holistic therapies, deep relaxation, and hypnosis, she sensed she was still working on the fringe.

"So many clients asked me about meditation that I decided to learn it myself so I could teach them. A few months ago, I began attending meditation and centering workshops. I learned how to meditate on a candle flame, on my breath, and guided imagery. But I confess that I still don't have a clue as to what meditation is really all about. What is meditation, and how and why does it work?"

D. Meditation means stilling the mind. Why do we still it? To know who we are. We are not the body or the mind. We are that limitless pure Consciousness that transcends both. We are existence itself, existence that does not depend on a period of time, a place, or a condition. We are absolute bliss, not the bliss evoked from contact with an object or person but pure unobjectified bliss. To realize THAT is why we meditate. To live in the sustained experience of THAT is called enlightenment or Self-realization. We do not meditate to get something we don't have. We meditate to know what we already are.

G. No one who taught me meditation ever explained it to me that way. What do I do now? How do I get that experience?

D. Give some thought to what motivates your clients, and what motivates most people to meditate. We are sick and tired of the uncontrolled flow of thought that enslaves us and keeps us hopping to fulfill every whim. We're sick of needing drugs to blast our minds out of existence. We're sick of hate, jealousy, fear, insecurity, and loneliness. At the root of it all is alienation from our Self, from our center. Distractions have run us out of our Home and cut us off from Source. Falsely, we identify with our ever-restless, ever-changing body and mind instead of the boundless Being we are. We want limitlessness. We want permanence. We want joy. For that, we have to transcend the mind.

An Indian master instructed seekers who wanted to learn meditation to ask themselves this question: What is my highest concept of Reality? Saturate that question with reflection because that Reality is what you want to tie into. What you meditate on you will experience, so your object should be what you want. Give yourself time to think about it. Meditation is a lifetime affair, not a one-shot session.

Suppose your highest concept of Reality is an Incarnation. In that case, your object of meditation is Reality in a personal form. Your culture and tradition will determine whether the form is Jesus, Krishna, Muhammad, Gautama Buddha, or other forms.

Suppose your highest concept of Reality is all-pervading Light, infinity, Being-ness, pure Intelligence, and formlessness. You would meditate on the impersonal Reality called Brahman in Sanskrit. If your highest concept of Reality is the I AM behind the name and form of Gail, you would meditate on your identity as the nondual Brahman. What is essential is that you understand and love what you meditate on. Your heart must be involved, not your head. Only the heart can penetrate that "cloud of unknowing."

G. Suppose I have my object clear in my mind. Where do I go from there?

D. Among the most scientific paths of spiritual development is Raja Yoga (the King's Yoga). Through eight rungs of the ladder called Ashtanga Yoga (Eight Steps), we can reach the zenith of human evolution. The first two steps focus on character and ethical purity. The third step is Hatha Yoga (postures). To meditate deeply, the body must be able to remain absolutely motionless. Yoga asanas bestow this inner poise. The fourth step is Pranayama (breath control). Slow, quiet breathing is a prerequisite for meditation. The fifth step is sense-withdrawal. Our senses must withdraw from objects before we can meditate. Most important is the sixth step, concentration, for without concentration, the seventh step, meditation, is impossible. Trying to meditate before working the first six steps is like putting a roof on a house before putting up the walls.

When meditation gets very deep, we enter the superconscious state. We cannot climb onto that eighth rung of the ladder. We are lifted up to it by the divine Force within.

You live in a big city where you have access to Hatha and Raja Yoga classes that teach according to ancient Eastern traditions. Take advantage of it. If you can find only Hatha Yoga instruction, then work the Eight Steps guided by good books on Raja Yoga. Systematic and simultaneous practice of the rungs of the Raja Yoga ladder will yield an understanding of Truth and the capacity to meditate deeply.

G. Will I be able to teach my clients to meditate?

D. Of course, and not only that. Every infusion from higher states of consciousness will transform you *and* your clients. After all, what we give to others is not what we know. We give them what we are.

Meditation:
What's Really Going On?

Richard's interests embraced the corporate world and the world of inner adventure. He was only eight years old when he learned about the I-Ching, Tarot cards, and Indian sweat lodges. His father taught yoga postures to him and his brothers; his mother urged him to develop his latent occult powers. When he was twenty-eight years old, he got a job with an American corporate giant researching New Age transformational technologies. The idea was to improve productivity by cutting through impedances that blocked it, not from the conventional approach of outside-in but through unorthodox methods of inside-out.

"So far," Richard told us, "meditation seems to have a more profound effect on people than anything else; it brings about an instant change. I've seen tense executives smile, relax, and let go, even after one sitting. I'd like to understand *why* this happens. I know, for example, that meditation brings blood pressure down dramatically, but I don't know how it does. What is really going on when a person meditates?"

D. If you want an explanation that the corporate world can relate to with ease, you can say that deep meditation brings about a synchronicity of right and left brain hemispheres. Experiencing synchronicity is experiencing oneness, a state of nonduality in which nothing is desired outside of oneself. You become complete, whole; a perfect integration and balance of male and female energies.

Another way to explain meditation is in terms of brain waves. Let's say you are sitting in your office. You don't know what to do first. Work is piled on your desk. The telephone is ringing. You are expected at a board room conference in ten minutes. Hungry, you dash to the snack room for a Coke. If an electroencephalograph (EEG) were attached to your head as you were running around, it might show a brain wave frequency of 22 cycles per second, the beta range.

When you get home, you take a shower, do a little reading, and then sit in your meditation seat. As you relax every part of your body and calm your mind, your brain wave frequency slows down to about 10 cycles per second, the alpha range. Now you begin to concentrate. All the rays of your consciousness are focused on your object of attention: a photo of the moon that you love, a statue of a great American Indian whose character you want to emulate, a mantra, a word, or a single idea. Your body sits motionless. No longer are you conscious of it. Nothing enters your consciousness—no distractions, no thoughts, only the object of your concentration. At this point, an EEG might measure a frequency in the theta range of about 4 cycles per second.

As an advanced student, your concentration attains perfection. You reach a state of absorption. Subject and object merge, and the object disappears. Nonduality is the essence of your experience. Perhaps an EEG would pick up a frequency of 2 cycles per second, the delta range. A dip into that peace and bliss dissolves anxiety and fear, and not just for a moment. The infusion can transform one's entire personality.

When your meditation deepens into superconscious

states beyond delta, you leave behind the world of brain-wave technology and corporate terminology. Metaphysically, what happens in deep meditation is that God knows himself; Self experiences itself.

R. I don't understand. Isn't it me, the man, who is knowing God?

D. A man cannot know God. Finite can never know the Infinite. Only the perceiver can perceive the perceiver.

R. Is this idea from a particular religious orientation?

D. This is neither an idea nor a religious orientation. This transcendence of body and mind, this dropping of the boundaries of the finite self, is an experience of advanced mystics from all traditions. St. Bernard wrote that "it is no merely human joy to lose oneself like this, . . . to be emptied of oneself as though one almost ceased to be at all. . . . How otherwise could God be 'all in all' if anything of man remained in man?" Augustine Baker wrote that the Christian contemplative "cometh to a pure and total abstraction, and then he seemeth to himself to be all spirit and as if he had no body . . ."

Zen master Han-Shan said, "Suddenly, I stood still, filled with the realization that I had no body or mind. All I could see was one great illuminating Whole— omnipresent, perfect, lucid and serene. . . . I felt clear and transparent." Dogen wrote that his mind and body dropped off in an ecstasy of release. Vedic sage Sri Ramana Maharshi explained that we are formless, that considering ourselves to have a form is the primal ignorance and the root cause of all our trouble. "In the superconscious state, the Self knows what it is, once and for all." The sustained experience of that state is called enlightenment.

R. How does the Self relate to the mind? Or does it have a relationship with it?

D. Self is the Witness of the mind.

R. If Self witnesses the mind, why do we need formal meditation?

D. Meditation introduces us to the Witness. Stated another way, meditation lifts the veil that obstructs our vision of what we truly are.

Money:
A Spiritual Perspective

Having recently left a Trappist monastery where he lived for three years, Victor was trying to adjust to secular life. "I can't find a job," he said, "not because I'm not capable. It's that my vow of poverty hangs over my head. Looking down on wealth and worldly success got ingrained in me. I don't know how to get it out."

D. Many exmonastics share your problem. Nor does one have to be a monastic to get this message. In the Bible it is written that it is harder for a rich man to get to God that it is for a camel to go through the eye of a needle. And who hasn't heard that money is the root of all evil?

I would like to share with you two meditation practices that might help you. Do you still meditate?

V. Sure. I would never drop that.

D. While you were in the monastery, what method did you use to root out attachments?

V. I offered them to God. Then I meditated on their uselessness or their harmful effects.

D. Clinging to poverty on a conscious or subconscious level is also an attachment. Many of us get attached to a life-style of poverty just as much as others get attached to wealth. To root out this attachment, meditate on the fact that the Lord has taken you out of the monastery and placed you in the world. Offer to him your attachment to poverty. Then meditate on the counterproductive effects of poverty in your new role.

This Eastern tale might clarify the point. King Janaka possessed great stores of wealth and ruled a huge kingdom, despite the fact that he was a realized soul. One day a wandering monk knocked on his door and asked the king to take a walk with him. King Janaka agreed. The king carried nothing. The monk carried his water bowl, the traditional symbol of a life of poverty. After they walked a short distance, the monk turned to the king. "If you want to realize God," he said, "you must renounce your gold, palace, dancing girls, court musicians, and your entire kingdom."

"Fine," said King Janaka. "I'll do it."

The monk looked surprised. "When?" he asked.

"Right now," said the king.

The monk was stunned. In silence they walked on. Suddenly a cheeky youngster ran out of the forest, grabbed the monk's water bowl, and ran away. The monk threw up his arms and shouted obscenities that the king had never before heard. King Janaka burst out laughing. "You have only a water bowl,' 'he said. "Yet you are more attached to your life-style and your bowl than I am to my entire kingdom."

In themselves, poverty and wealth are neither evil nor good. Our minds imbue them with qualities that do not inhere in them. Like a spider getting caught in the web it spins, we get locked in the prisons that our minds create. To escape, you have to erase the old tapes that your mind still plays, and update them to accord with your current reality.

Sri Aurobindo's view of money makes a good replacement tape. He says that money is a symbol of universal force: "When spiritual people renounce wealth, they leave the power in the hands of hostile forces. To reconquer it for the Divine to whom it belongs and use it divinely for the divine purpose is the way of this yoga." He advises us neither to shrink from the power of money nor to become its slave. We are to regard ourselves as trustees of money, to use it selflessly and scrupulously, to offer it to the Divine Mother for her purposes and not for our own or for those of others.

Deep meditation on these new values should root out your attachment to poverty by freeing you from an ascetic withdrawal. It should also free you from getting bound by a sense of want if poverty continues, and by the desire for more if wealth comes along.

V. How long should the transformation take?

D. That depends on the degree and intensity of your commitment to change.

V. Why should change be so hard?

D. We are all on stage reading a script. Most of us identify intimately with the role we are given. That makes it hard to play the next role, especially when the script is very different. Shakespeare spilled the beans when he said that all the world is a stage. The bean he did not spill is that God alone is the actor.

Past:
Reality Lies Only in the Now

Twenty-three-year-old Neville came to my workshop on "Human Relationships and Spiritual Healing." He worked in a health food store in a small artists' colony town. Twice a week, he met with a group of friends to discuss Edgar Cayce's teachings. About two years before he attended the workshop, he lost his parents in a crash of their private plane. Months later, he discovered that Al, his twin brother, had lied to their parents about him and had manipulated them into leaving Neville out of their will. Al inherited their entire estate.

"When that fact came to light, I wanted to kill him," Neville said. "If it hadn't been for my Cayce friends, I would have done it. My hatred has abated somewhat, but it's still there. Al has a home, a Cadillac, and a beautiful woman. And I'm knocking my brains out to pay my rent.

"My Cayce friends said that I must have done something terrible to him to merit what he did to me. That thought helped me a lot. If you deserve something, then it's easier to accept it. Some weeks ago, I saw an ad for past life regressions. It costs a fortune, but perhaps it's worth it. I've got to know what I did to Al to bring this on. My question is: How far back can these past life regressionists take me?"

D. They can take you to the deepest recesses of their imagination and your bank account. Some of them charge hefty fees and do not even believe in reincarnation.

But suppose you go to one. Let's say that he or she tells you about the terrible thing you did to the entity who has become your brother. That might devastate you. In *Many Mansions*, author Dr. Gina Cerminara relates a reading of Cayce's on a man who had been Nero. Cayce did not tell the man about his past because he knew he could not cope with it. You, too, might be unable to cope with what you hear. Soon you would wonder what Al could have done to you to cause you to commit such an act. On and on it would go. No beginning, no end.

Another problem with such a past-life focus is confusion. Your brother may have been your father or your son. When we experience a different past relationship with someone in our current scenario, life becomes confusing. How should you relate to this woman in your bed who once bore you in her womb?

N. Would you say that Cayce's work is useless?

D. On the contrary. Edgar Cayce was a phenomenon. Through his extraordinary powers of clairvoyance, he prescribed, diagnosed, and cured people throughout the world of physical and mental ailments that defied conventional medicine. Cayce never read past lives to appease idle curiosity or to get rich. He did it only to alleviate suffering. But we must face this fact: the Edgar Cayces of our world are very, very few and very far apart!

N. Then how shall I deal with this anger in me?

D. Take Cayce's teachings to a deeper level in

yourself. Talking about them is one thing, but unless we meditate on them, they will not transform us. Reflect on the fact that Al is reading from a script that he did not write. The script is based on the law. Behind the law stands the Director. By leaning on the Director's arm, Cayce says, our consciousness changes, for he is Truth and Light. We find the Director's arm by learning to surrender to all that happens to us, by knowing that whatever occurs does so for our ultimate good. As for the law, we must accept the fact that it is just. We should not fight it, but trust that every payment asked of us is the right price for a debt we incurred.

Life passes quickly. Enslaved by desire and fear, we dwell on the past and dream of the future, and we miss the whole point. The point is the present. That is all we have and that is all we are. Past is memory. Future is imagination. Reality lies only in the now.

Prayer:
Heartless Words or
a Wordless Heart

Widowed Elizabeth, who worked as a secretary for a
motor vehicle bureau, told us that praying did nothing
for her life. ''For twenty-five years I've gone to
church,'' she said. ''When I walk out of church I'm
the same person as when I walked in. My prayers and
motions are mechanical and dry. How can I change
this?''

D. Pray with your heart.

E. I don't know how.

D. Have you ever been in love? While you were in
love, your mind did not have to be taught how to meditate on your beloved. Your heart knew. Your heart
functioned in high gear with no instruction. Real prayer
is just like that. You don't dictate to your heart. The
heart calls the shots itself.

Here is the way to start. First, you need a very clear
concept of your ideal. To get that, write down everything you know, feel, or believe to be true about God.
Your list will come from your own understanding, from
your highest concept of Reality. It might include such
words as omnipotence, omnipresence, love, all-pervading Light, infinity, compassion, mercy, purity, and

peace. You might wish to narrow your list down to six primary words or even three.

When you finish the list, set up a meditation seat in a quiet corner of your home where you can sit undisturbed when you get up and before you go to bed. Relax your body, and look at your list. Mentally repeat one word at a time. Project it onto the screen of your consciousness the way you would project film onto a movie screen. As you repeat the word, dwell on your deepest understanding of its essence. On their own accord, the repetitions will soon cease, and you will be established in your wordless center, your heart.

To pray with the heart and no words is much better than to pray with words and no heart.

Prayer for Change:
Pray for a Raincoat,
Not for the Sun

Widowed Dorothy, who meditated and prayed regularly, had worked in a government office for eighteen years. Recently, she was transferred to a department where the staff was half her age. Many of them were irresponsible, she said. They argued constantly and left incomplete tasks on her desk.

Three times a day, she prayed for change, but the change had not come. "I can't understand why my prayers go unheeded," she told us. "I'm desperate! My circumstances are all wrong—the people, the work, the place. Yet I can't find another job. Somebody told me that prayer would not help, but occult practices would. That's what I'd like to ask you about."

D. Occult practices can bring you into contact with powers that may have more of an adverse effect on your life than your current circumstances. Prayer *can* help if you understand its dynamics.

Recognize, first of all, that your placement in those circumstances is neither wrong nor accidental. Everything has a purpose: people we meet, places we're put, events that occur in our lives. To get beyond any unpleasant situation, we have to go through it. The trick is to pass through it in a state of inner surrender without a battle. The key to that is to meet each circumstance as though it were specially designed for you—because it was. Our delightful and rotten circumstances are schools designed to teach us specific lessons. They may not be easy but altering our angle of vision this way can help.

An effective way to invite a change of circumstances is a prayer of surrender like this: "Lord, if it be your will, remove me to a place where I can function harmoniously." After the prayer, meditate in silence on peace and love, and drop all thought of your problems. Letting go creates a vacuum in which a change can take place. The problem with praying from a negative inner state is that it impedes the flow of grace.

You can close your meditation with this prayer: "Lord, if this change is not your Will, if this rain is going to keep pouring down on me, then I won't ask you for the sun. Just give me the best raincoat that you've got!"

Relationships:
Three Spiritual Guidelines

Divorced three times and planning to marry again, Mame sought guidelines at my workshop on "Human Relationships and the Spiritual Way." "When I am on my own," she said, "life runs smoothly. As soon as I get close to someone, problems start—disappointment, disillusionment. It happens like clockwork."

D. Why?

M. People don't measure up to my expectations. My last husband, for example, would forget everything that was important to me—evenings that we planned together, simple groceries, even my birthday. That was ample proof that I didn't matter to him.

D. Many years ago I knew a man who never forgot my birthday or the anniversary of our meeting or anything I asked him.

M. That's the sign of sincerity that I want.

D. That's only a sign of a good memory. He remembered not only *my* birthday; he also remembered the birthdays of three other women he dated at the same time. I share this with you to show you that our expectations of others have no basis in reality.

The first spiritual guideline to healthy relationships is to neutralize all expectations. Grasp the fact that each

144

of us acts according to an inner blueprint. Just as you cannot act, feel, or think as others would like you to, you cannot design their behavior. As the *Bhagavad Gita* puts it, we are entitled to the action but not to the fruit.

M. I don't understand.

D. Let's say you cook a five-course meal. You do the best you can, and you do it with love. Your husband comes home, doesn't say thank you, and doesn't even feel like eating. How would you react?

M. I would get upset and start to think, "What's wrong? Did he take another woman out to dinner? The least he could do is acknowledge my efforts!"

D. If you were living according to spiritual laws, your reaction would differ. You would accept his response without reading anything into it or viewing it as a judgment of your worth.

M. But how can I deal with my thoughts?

D. Bring God into your life. That is the second spiritual guideline. Cultivate the inner attitude, "Let happen what will. I need no pat on the back. I expect nothing. All I do is for the Divine alone. Whether others hate it, love it, or ignore it is not my business. It is theirs."

M. But my thoughts overwhelm me.

D. Why should you let them? Watch them as an observer. When you hear your mind say, "Why doesn't he act like I want him to?" refuse to identify with that. Say to your mind, "There you go again. This time I'm not buying your old tape." Eventually, your unruly thoughts will lose their hold on you. Our problems come from our minds, not from other people. When we learn how to stand back and watch the mind's antics, our relationships improve dramatically.

The third spiritual guideline is to root your relationships in the Divine. Picture two couples walking along a road. The first couple, A and B, keep looking at one

145

another for their happiness. When B lets A down, A gets angry. That angers B, who feels that A is demanding. The second couple, C and D, walk hand in hand, but their eyes are not on one another. They are fixed on their common goal ahead—God-realization. Whatever happens—changes of mood in C or D, surprises, illness, disturbances, failures, irritations—their equanimity and peace remain intact. C and D have their roots in God, they walk towards God, and they support one another spiritually and morally in their common quest.

Kahlil Gibran put this idea beautifully. I suggest you meditate on his words:

Love one another but make not a bond of love
Let it rather be a moving sea between the shores of your souls....
Give your hearts but not into each other's keeping
For only the Hand of Life can contain your hearts
And stand together yet not too near together
For the pillars of the temple stand apart
And the oak tree and cypress grow not in each other's shadow.

Renunciation:
Denial or Transformation?

Doctors predicted that Sydney's congenital and "incurable" circulatory disease would shorten his life span to eighteen years. A chance meeting with a yoga teacher when he was fifteen saved him. Now twenty-nine, Sydney lives normally, writes scripts for television shows, and does two hours of yoga and meditation every day. Recently, his spiritual teacher told him that only through renunciation is progress possible.

D. Renunciation of what?

S. That's what troubles me. I guess she meant renunciation of everything I like. I'm still young. My girlfriend and I plan to marry, get a home, and start a family. I love my work. It looks as if I have a good career ahead of me. How can I give these things up? Yet I want to make spiritual progress. Can I somehow reconcile these conflicting desires? Or is reconciliation impossible?

D. Growing up with no brothers or sisters to play games with, I spent many hours with dolls. Dolls from all over the world adorned my room. For hours every day my imagination had free play as I projected whole universes onto my dolls.

Years passd, and I got interested in other things—

arithmetic, geography, and music. One day, in the corner of my closet, I saw a box I hadn't noticed for a long time. I opened it and was surprised; there must have been a hundred dolls in it. That day I gave all of them to the younger kids on our street. I had never told myself or my parents that thenceforth I would renounce dolls. When other things engaged my attention, my interest in dolls dropped like an overripe fruit.

Spiritual life is like that. As we ripen, whatever is unnecessary drops away by itself. Until that happens, why should we knock all the apples off the tree? We should deal with them as best we can but try not to accrue any more.

S. But how do I make progress without renouncing?

D. No one can, but what matters is the object of renunciation. To make certain and speedy progress, we need to renounce our sense of do-ership. I will share with you two approaches to this practice of renunciation.

The first and easier way is Karma Yoga. Most people live their lives and carry on their work motivated by a desire for money, success, name, fame, power, pleasure, or the need for self-expression. In Karma Yoga these motives are replaced by the desire to consecrate one's entire life to God, to want nothing for oneself.

Rabbi Zalman Schachter describes the initial steps in his book, *The First Step*. This process hinges on the Hebrew word *Kavvanah*, meaning "intention." "Our intention is always free. For instance, you sit in the dentist's chair. He drills and you feel a sting of pain, but you can 'intend' this pain as an offering of love. . . . 'Ribbono Shel Olam! You are good and Your universe is good. The all is filled with Your mercy and goodness, as is the pain I feel. . . . Please accept this moment of pain as a love offering from me.' Or you travel...lean back...and say, 'Sweet Father, I enjoy Your presence...the rhythm of the wheels, the fleeting scenery, all are nothing but You.' " All these "arrows of awareness," the Rabbi writes, "will place us in the presence of God."

The second approach is the way of Jnana Yoga, the path of knowledge. On this path, you witness rather than identify with the drama taking place. Players include Sydney, your fiancée, and colleagues. Props are offices, home, classes, and plans. You are reading the script a line at a time. On this path, you renounce your sense of do-ership by perceiving, through meditation, that Sydney is not writing his script or planning his plot. You renounce the sense that Sydney is an individual agent of action, a separate ego bound by a bag of skin.

S. How can I experience that I am not the agency of action?

D. Through meditation and self-enquiry. In your spare moments throughout the day, ask yourself, "On what screen is this personal drama being projected? Who is perceiving it? To whom or to what is it happening?"

S. What does that reflection do?

D. Two things. First, it allows the drama to flow freely, unimpeded by Sydney's superimposed ambition, fear, and anxiety, all of which plant seeds for a relentless procession of dramas. Second, it lifts you beyond the level of drama-identification. The greater your constancy of focus on your identity as pure unattached Awareness behind the show, the speedier your progress will be.

Spiritual progress means narrowing the gulf between who we think we are and who we really are. Try with all your might to dispel the belief that you are the limited player-form called Sydney. Books such as *I Am*

That by Sri Nisargadatta and the works of Sri Ramana Maharshi and Sri Swami Sivananda will help you to grasp the fact that you are not a limited form: you are the formless, silent, supreme and infinite backdrop on which all the dramas of life take place.

S. I always thought that renunciation meant dumping your attachments and trekking off to a monastery.

D. In the past, that is what it meant. Today's seekers cannot dump their families and take off for solitude. We have to bring the monastery into our hearts. Renunciation of the world was the key to spiritual progress. Today, the key is transformation.

Seekers' Guidelines:
Everything Is Food

For five years after turning twenty-three, Stanley lived in an ashram in upstate New York. A conflict with the swami-in-charge ended in his departure and a loss of faith. Now he sought to make sense of it all.

"There are so many *dos* and *don'ts*," Stanley said. "Don't watch TV. Don't read novels. Don't wear polyester. Don't hang out with worldly people. What an unnecessary regulation of our lives! Is it not enough to get up early, meditate, and stick to a vegetarian diet?"

D. *Everything* is food, not merely what you chew in your mouth and digest in your stomach. In P. D. Ouspensky's *In Search of the Miraculous*, Gurdjieff explains that air and impressions are also food. Sounds that enter our ears, sights we see, objects we smell, taste, and touch, objects that touch us, and thoughts that enter our minds from forces near and far—all are food. These foods consist of force fields that impinge upon and alter the force fields that flow through and around us.

From your studies with the swami, you probably learned that we have three bodies: physical, subtle, and causal. Every food force that we take in also has three bodies. Its grossest dimension feeds our gross body; its subtle dimension feeds our subtle body; its causal dimension feeds our causal body. Whether we are conscious of it or not, at every moment of our lives, the forces we imbibe are feeding all the planes of our existence.

An orthodox rabbi once told me something interesting that relates to this idea. He said that written in a Hebrew scripture is this dictum: "When you go to see a holy man, do not wear a garment of mixed fibers." The rabbi did not know the reason for this injunction. Sages in the East would say that in the presence of a master, one should make oneself as receptive as possible to the master's fields of force. For example, one's body should be still, one's mind silent. One should eat nothing and wear nothing that would adversely affect the reception of those finer forces.

Spiritual seekers try to attune themselves to the highest possible vibrations, to subtle and powerful forces. So the most important aspect of spiritual work is purification: preparing both body and mind to receive higher forms of energy.

Do's and *don'ts* help weed out harmful foods in myriads of forms. To the extent that we consciously control our intake, to that extent we progress. If we do not take such measures, we may move one step forward in an hour's meditation, and six steps backwards for the next twenty-three hours. It would be like pouring water into a bucket with a big hole in the bottom.

Self-Realization:
You Can't Be Half-Realized

By day, Jason worked as a commercial artist. At night, in the loft above his private studio, he sat for long periods of time in Vedantic meditation with the mantra, So Ham (That I Am). Systematically, he had studied Vedantic scriptures, such as the *Atma Bodha* (Self-Knowledge) and the principal *Upanishads*. Jason came to the workshop seeking clarity on the state of Realization.

"Sometimes I understand the subtlest truths with great clarity," he told us. "But at the same time, I know I haven't gone all the way. Could I possibly have reached a state of being half-realized?"

D. Water begins to boil only at a specific point, not before. Realization is similar. The sages say that it is like waking up from sleep. Waking has no half-measures. Nobody needs to confirm to us the fact that we have awakened. Experience alone confirms it. Sri Swami Krishnananda says that when the knower has awakened, he no longer sees objects as objects. In his awakened state, the entire universe of objects dissolves into a totality of Subjectness. The late Thomas Merton, a Trappist monk, had the same experience in a Kentucky town near his monastery. Everything he looked at—a person, a pillar, a dog—*everything*—he saw as God.

No matter how deep our intellectual understanding, until we perceive oneness within and without, we are like water on the stove that has not begun to boil.

Self-Realization:
How Long Does It Take?

Twenty-three-year-old Sandy wanted enlightenment, and she wanted it fast. For the past two years while working in a printing press, she spent all her spare time and thought on Tibetan Buddhist practices. Nothing else interested her.

"I want to know how long enlightenment takes," she said. "I asked several people, and I got different answers from all of them."

D. Eastern scriptures say that it takes as long to become enlightened as it does to blink an eye or to see a fruit in the palm of one's hand. Enlightenment actually means "waking up," which takes an instant. But you are probably asking how long the preparation takes. Three primary factors determine that. The first one is clarity of goal and method. It is like going on a journey. You have to know exactly where you are headed and how you are going to get there. A second factor is the starting point. Suppose both of us want to go to Rome. You start out from Milan; I start from Miami. Almost certainly, you will reach Rome first, and you'll reach Rome fast.

The third factor is intensity of yearning. Let's say that both of us start taking piano lessons. I just want to learn to play, so I practice twenty minutes a day. But you want to perform Tchaikovsky's Piano Concerto in Carnegie Hall next year. On some days, when my friends ask me to go mountain climbing or bowling, I don't practice at all. On the other hand, you practice five hours every day. You never miss. You refuse social invitations and dates that take you away from the piano. Even on your morning walks, you memorize phrases of the concerto. The goal never leaves you. With such intensity of yearning, your period of preparation will be short.

S. That is what I wanted to hear. You see, I haven't got much time. I'm scared that my karma might start coming down on my head before I'm ready, before I get enlightenment.

Sandy burst into tears and cried for several minutes. Then she told us that when she turned eighteen she got a job tending bar. During her three years as a bartender, she became addicted to cocaine and heroin and peddled them for a while. One Sunday afternoon, her boyfriend brought her to a university auditorium to hear a visiting Tibetan Buddhist monk from Nepal.

"The moment he started talking, something happened to me," she said. "I got scared. He was talking about karma. Nobody had to tell me he was right. I knew it. He talked about how you can't change what you've done. You've got to pay for it, every bit of it, the way you have to pay your debts. He also said that we have an obligation to free ourselves from the prison of body and mind.

"I sat there thinking of the terrible things I did. I got scared as hell. I was still into drugs then, and some of the stuff I was doing was base. My God, I thought, what will happen to me?

"When the talk was over, I rushed down to talk to him. Instead of asking him anything, I burst into tears.

Somebody ushered me into a room behind the stage while the monk talked with people there. When he finished, he came back to me. No words came out of me. In his presence, I felt like I was Home. I was still scared. But I knew that he had or that he was something I could hold onto. I told him just a little, that I did terrible things. But I gave him no details.

"He gave me explicit instructions for spiritual practices and said I must start that very night. He also gave me a mantra to repeat. When I got home, I turned over a new leaf. Since then, I've been out of the drug scene. I got a job with a printing press, and I don't hang out with the drug crowd anymore. I sleep from 10:00 to 4:00 as he told me to do. I don't eat at night, and I don't eat flesh food. My meditation and other practices are regular. I wish I could see him or write, but I don't know where he is. All I want to tell him is that I'm still scared, just like I was from day one."

D. Ordinary fears are harmful. Your fear is *not* ordinary. Mystical traditions call the fear of God or of God's law "the first great gift." In *The Philokalia*, we read that those who quail with such fear are inexpressibly contrite in soul: "For the Lord has established this as the basic commandment knowing that without this even heaven is profitless," and, "No one can love God [or the highest state of Consciousness, the goal of your practices] unless he has first feared him with all his heart. Through the action of fear, the soul is purified and...awakens to the action of love."

Your fear functions as an extraordinary fillip to your practices. That fear motivates you. It is driving you forward to levels of spirituality you could never reach without it.

Please read the story of Milarepa, a Tibetan Buddhist who had practiced black magic before he met his guru. Like you, he became terrified by what he had done.

Overwhelming fear of the results of his actions drove him into perfect discipleship, and finally to enlightenment.

Once you become established in your practices, the fear will leave you. In other words, your fear will remain with you only as long as you need it.

Rome may not be far off.

Spiritual Experience:
Chase the Experiencer,
Not the Experience

As a minister for many years of a mainline Protestant church, Joe introduced meditation to his congregation. "As I see it," he said, "that is the only way their hearts will open up to Jesus." His pull towards meditation began on the morning he sat in a small empty chapel on the east coast. Through the windows, he saw the ocean and heard the roar of waves. His thoughts stopped, and suddenly an intense white light engulfed him and held him suspended in a breathless state of ecstasy. "That was the first time I understood what Jesus is," he told us.

That had happened eight years ago. Since then, Joe had sat in the new meditation room of his house for many hours and gone back often to that little chapel in order to see the light again. "But it doesn't come. That is the most frustrating part of it. Eight years, and it hasn't returned. I'd appreciate some insight into why it won't come back when I try so hard."

D. It won't come back *because* you try so hard. When you sit for meditation, what do you think about?

J. I think about that light, how exquisite it was, what it made me feel, and how much I want it.

D. That is what stands in your way. Desiring any-

159

thing in meditation introduces the element of *rajas*—restless activity. That precludes experience.

J. How did the light come in the first place?

D. Your mind was still. According to what you said, the sound and sight of the ocean had a strong impact on you. It stirred your heart and stilled your mind. You opened yourself and the experience came.

J. Please explain what *rajas* means.

D. Rajas is one of the three universal forces (''gunas'' in Sanskrit) that govern our lives. Some teachers describe them as qualities. Yet they are the stuff of life as much as strands of a rope are the stuff of the rope: *Tamas* is passivity or inertia, *rajas* is action or restlessness, and *sattwa* is harmony or purity.

J. How do they affect our lives?

D. When tamas preponderates, we want to sleep; tamas is the cause of our resistance to getting out of bed in the morning. When rajas predominates, our bodies and minds want to be active. Rajas hinders meditation. We may feel peace, but if our mind is rajasic it will nudge us, ''Let's get up now—enough of this sitting-still business.'' When sattwa predominates, we meditate well. The best time to meditate is when sattwa prevails in the atmosphere, an hour and a half before dawn and before dusk. If we meditate then, the universal forces support us.

J. Getting back to my question—it is wrong, then, to desire light?

D. Not wrong, just counterproductive. Desire for experience brings on rajas and defeats our purpose.

J. What puzzles me is that spiritual experiences whet your appetite for them. You want more.

D. I have heard it said that experiences are given to us, often to beginners, to provide faith in what we are doing.

J. How should we regard such experiences if we are not to be encouraged to want them again?

D. Like all experience—as a parade of passing phenomena. What does not last is not real. Reality lies only in the Giver of gifts.

J. Can we nevertheless make practical use of such experiences, in sermons, for example?

D. Why not? Perhaps this is why it was given to you. Many Christians turn to the East because they want spiritual experience. Your experience will inspire them.

J. Have you any suggestions for my meditation in the future?

D. Wanting nothing, recalling nothing, seeking nothing, open your heart to the love of Jesus. Through its impact, you may hear the gentle murmur of his words: "Be still and know that I am God."

Spiritual Growth:
A Subtractive Process

A young doctor of holistic medicine from New York City was inquisitive. The revitalizing effects of meditation on the body and the mind were easy for him to grasp, as was the goal of "revelation," as he put it. But Brian could not understand the transformative process in which meditation plays only one part. "If we are already that boundless Spirit," he asked, "why must we work so hard to know it? I am a doctor. I don't have to go transform myself to know that I'm one. Why must the spiritual process be so different?"

D. The attainment of Self-Realization or revelation, as you put it, is the subtlest of all processes. You can liken it to climbing a high mountain. At the top, the air is more rarefied than below. You must climb steadily but slowly so that your lungs and other body systems can accommodate the changes in the atmosphere.

A heavy backpack weighs you down when you start out. After a while, you realize that you need to shed some of the load. Everything you can do without, you get rid of. A while later, perhaps a third of the way up, the climb gets harder, so you let go of still more things that you can do without.

The spiritual path is like a mountain path. We have

to shed all things that turn our attention outward and keep us focused on the unreal. The first things to go are physical redundancies, such as nonessential possessions and habits of excess sleep, excess food, and idle talk. After shedding the clutter in our spaces, we shed the clutter in our time. No longer do we waste precious hours with people, interests, and things that steer us from our goal.

At this point, we begin to lift the veil that makes our minds dense. Judgments, concepts, and preferences must go. Finally, the planning faculty falls away, and our sense of doership dissolves. Stripped of that baggage, we can climb with a light step at a good pace.

The process, then, does not require any gymnastics that are foreign to us. Rather than accruing or adding something, the spiritual process is subtractive, a debrainwashing that reveals our true nature. When we clean dross off a light bulb, the light shines with full luminosity. Dross is our baggage. The bulb is the mind. The light is the Self.

After subtracting the dross and confusion of what we are not, we live in the fullness of what we are.

Spiritual Progress:
An Unfailing Criterion

The thirty-five-year-old architectural draftsman had been going to yoga and meditation classes for the past three years. "In all other disciplines, results are tangible," Stuart said. "But the spiritual path is different. How do I know whether I am *really* making progress? In architecture, I know it in no uncertain terms. But what yardstick can I use to determine whether I'm going forward on the spiritual path?"

D. The yardstick of spiritual progress is as tangible as the one for architecture. Ask yourself this question: "What does it take to throw me off? Whenever you feel annoyed, irritated, angry, or depressed, make a note of what provoked it, how much feeling you manifested, and how long the feeling stayed with you. After three months, look at your notes. Compare your state of mind. Do you react to the same provocations with less emotion now than you did three months back? If so, you are making progress. Your meditation is working for you. If, however, you react to disagreeable circumstances like humiliation, blame, and so-called failure with the same emotion or more emotion than you did three months back, then you are going in the wrong direction. Also, consider your overreactions to praise and ego-inflation.

Beneath this visible criterion is the operation of a spiritual dynamic: surrender. Your Hatha Yoga, pranayama, and meditation purify your body and your mind, the "sheaths" that surround the Self. The greater the purification, the more apparent it becomes that the Universal Intelligence is running the show and that Stuart is not. That discovery triggers the spiritual dynamic of surrender that is pivotal to progress. The greater your inner surrender, the less your outer emotional reaction to praise, blame, love, hate, failure, and success. Surrender means letting go, and letting go means inner peace. The steadiness of your inner peace is the unfailing criterion of spiritual progress.

Spiritual Success:
An Instant Formula

Trudy, a divorcee, was thirty-six when her mother died. Left with a sizable inheritance, she turned her home into a modest ashram. In her yoga room, she practices asanas (postures), pranayama (breath control), and meditation for three hours every morning and evening. During the day, she teaches yoga.

"One of the books I follow says that for Self-Realization one must meditate six hours every day," she said. "Right now I can sit in one posture for one and a half hours at a time. If I double this time to three hours at each sitting, how fast can I attain the superconscious state?"

D. Someone once asked a Vedic master in the Himalayas the same question. He answered, "By itself, meditation for six or even nine hours a day will not suffice. If you want fast enlightenment, I will give you an easy instant formula: Think of God twenty-four hours a day."

What the master meant was that the success of spiritual efforts depends not merely on length, regularity, and depth of meditation. It depends more on the degree to which the thought of God permeates our entire day.

Surrender:
The Secret of
Self-Transformation

Phil and Brenda drove a long way to the workshop on "Surrender—Let Go and Let God." Married for thirty-five years, they lived most of that time in their ancestral home in New Jersey. Costly heirlooms had filled their home—oil paintings, ivory statues, gold dinner sets—until their two-week holiday in Florida a year before. Then their house was broken into and all the heirlooms were stolen. The loss affected Phil's health, and Brenda broke down. "Counsellors keep telling us that we must learn to surrender," Phil said, "but we don't know how."

D. Surrender means letting go of the fiction that you are an independent agent of action, and that others are independent agents of action—thieves or saints. The universe is a play of Consciousness. The Universal Mind which inheres in the Supreme Consciousness creates, maintains, and dissolves all there is. In other words, God, that nameless formless existence, has taken the form of the universe and all that is in it. Only when you know that in your heart, can you surrender.
P. How does knowing that help us surrender?
D. When that knowledge pervades your heart and mind and life, you know with absolute certitude that

everything happens for a reason and for your ultimate good. You stop fighting life when you know that a cosmic force is behind it all, and not an individual person.

P. Why is surrender so hard for most people?

D. For us Westerners, surrender is a cultural problem. It doesn't go with getting ahead of the Joneses or with the idea that if things don't happen you've got to make them happen.

P. But isn't that true? Don't we have to make things happen?

D. The answer to that depends on the inner place from which you look at it. When things have to happen and when they have to happen through us, then we do what has to be done. Our mistake is that we think it is we—Darshani, Phil, Brenda—who *make* them happen.

P. But aren't we all different from one another, different people with different things to do?

D. We are microcosmic links on a macrocosmic chain, or microcosmic cells in the macrocosmic body. That Cosmic Body is the aggregate of all individual bodies; and the Cosmic Mind is the aggregate of all individual minds.

Let's say you are sitting at home on your easy chair. Your foot gets a cramp. Instantly your entire body responds with discomfort. You stretch out your foot and move it around until the discomfort goes. Your foot did not act as a separate agent of action. Signals in your brain and nervous system triggered its movement. Cosmic impulses arise in us in a similar way. Mistakenly, we appropriate their authorship to ourselves.

P. It seems to me that such a philosophy would make people very passive, submissive, in fact.

D. Surrender, as you may know, is the key to the conversion of many alcoholics. Dr. Harry Tiebout, a researcher on alcoholism, wrote an article about that point some years ago. He said that "in submission, an individual accepts. . .as a practical fact that he cannot at that moment conquer reality, but lurking in his unconscious is the feeling, 'There'll come a day—' which implies no real acceptance and demonstrates conclusively that the struggle is still going on.

"When, on the other hand, [surrender] the ability to accept reality, functions on the unconscious level, there is no residual battle, and relaxation ensues with freedom from strain and conflict. In fact, it is perfectly possible to ascertain to what extent the acceptance of reality is on the unconscious level by the degree of relaxation which develops. The greater the relaxation, the greater is the inner acceptance of reality." So you see, we function much more productively and efficiently when we surrender.

P. What would Brenda and I be like if we had attained a high degree of surrender to God?

D. You would have little or no emotional reaction to the theft. Instead, you would regard the loss with purposeful knowing that nothing happens without a reason. You would sense that the loss may have occurred to teach you the folly of being attached to objects.

This story illustrates the point. In their eighties, Sol and Judy still lived on their century-old farm out west. Their only item of value was Judy's gold necklace, her prized possession. One day a stranger broke in, grabbed her necklace, and bolted off. Judy got hysterical. Sol, however, a highly evolved soul, smiled inwardly. He believed in the Bible. He knew that nothing could happen without the will of God—not even a hair could fall from his head. Still, to appease his wife, Sol pursued the thief. When he caught up with him and looked him in the eye, the thought of Judy left him instantly. All he saw was God playing the role of a thief. Sol knew in his heart that he could not change the Lord's script.

"Listen to me!" he said, wagging his forefinger at the thief. "That necklace cost $2000! Don't you sell it for one penny less!"

Will:
Life Is a Poker Game

Trevor, a bachelor thirty-two years of age, managed
an interchurch retreat center in Pennsylvania. He had
lived there for seven years, meditating and doing yoga
asanas. A year before, he had incorporated the discipline of acquiring virtues. He tried to cultivate a different virtue every forty days.

"What confuses me," Trevor told us, "is this problem of free will. Do we or don't we have it? If our stage
is set by the law of karma, then what play of will can
we have? Theoretically, I have none. Practically speaking, I do. I decide, for example, which people to book
into a double room, to whom to give a single room,
and what to cook. Small decisions are always coming
up, like the other night for instance.

"A large church group came for the weekend. Their
minister asked them to observe silence, to read, to contemplate, and to pray. About 10 P.M., I checked the
downstairs rooms. There in the sitting room were four
of the men playing poker! I closed the door, and for
some minutes, I stood there and deliberated. What
should I do? Should I tell them that they're here for
God and not cards? Should I remind them that their
minister said 'lights out at ten'? Or what? I prayed:
'Lord, tell me what to do.' Then I kept my mind free

of thought. Suddenly, a clear impulse rose within me to leave them alone. I walked off, knowing that the impulse came from a source higher than my mind. That instance was the exception to the rule. Most of the time, it strikes me that the decisions are 'mine.'

"If everything is already lined up, if it really is not me who makes the decisions, then what is there for me to do? What is my job in life?"

D. Life is like a poker game. We've all been dealt a hand of cards. God himself cannot change that hand. Let's say you've got the ten, the queen, the king, and the ace of spades. All you need for a royal flush is the jack of spades. How perfect that would be! But how sad! You've got the three of hearts instead.

All you need is that one government contract, and you'd be on millionaire's row. All you need for that beauty contest is a little plastic surgery: a pug nose would do it. All that's missing from your life is a new Honda, a thinner waistline, or the job that Bill has (which should have been given to you anyway because you have more on the ball than he does).

But the facts remain: Bill got the job (and his grass is no greener than yours). Mary won the beauty prize (she was more peaceful before). Jim has the Honda (somebody just ran into it, and the repair cost him a thousand bucks more than it would have on his old Chevy). The Honda, the pug nose, the government contract, and Bill's job are in the cards that were dealt to Bill, Jim, and Mary. They were and are not in your cards, for reasons you may never know. Yet the Law never works by chance.

Our job in life, as you put it, is twofold: One, to play the hand we've got with as much equanimity and honesty as we can. Equanimity means accepting the fact with our whole mind and heart that we have the three of hearts and not the jack of spades. It means

172

offering no resistance whatsoever to the fact that our hand is not a royal flush despite the fact that it misses by only a hair's breadth. It means allowing whatever happens to happen without kicking.

In other words, we are doing our job well when we drop all clinging to conditions or aims that we think would be much better than those dealt to us. We win the game not when we take the kitty on the table but when we trust totally in the wisdom and purposes of the Hand that dealt the cards.

Our second job is to stand back, abiding in Source, knowing that we are self-luminous awareness.

T. In other words, you can say that our job description reads "surrender" and "stand back."

D. Quite so. The bird of spiritual progress flies on these two wings. In surrender lie your freedom of will and your road to freedom.

T. How would I apply that idea to a practical situation? Suppose, for example, the same church group returns, and the same four guys play poker again. How do I apply what you said to that situation? What should I do?

D. We should never try to use one yardstick for all situations because situations vary. Let the Force within guide your response just as your guidance prompted you to leave the men alone. Our duty is not to be loyal to consistency; it is to be loyal to Truth as truth unfolds.

But for what it's worth, here is a suggestion. Let's say you are making your nightly rounds. Downstairs, you open the door to the sitting room. There they are, the four poker players. You get a green prompt from within. Sensing you are not unwelcome, you walk in slowly, pull up a chair, and smile. You might say, "Since you are playing cards, my friends, I would like to share a private thought with you. As I see it, life is like a poker game...."

Witness:
Shift Your Focus and Transform Your Life

Rob, a mid-forties business executive whose work was hampered by an ulcer, said he had been to many personal growth workshops. "What they tell me to do is to stand back from my negative emotions and to look at them," he said. "I've tried to do it, but I can't. Can you describe the process of separating yourself?"

D. Let's suppose you are walking alone through the woods, and you see a poisonous snake on your path. You shrink back, overcome by fear. The fear doesn't help, of course. It deprives you of your presence of mind. At this point, you shift your inner attention from the snake to your fear, which rises in the body in the region just below the navel. You are not looking at your body; you are observing your fear, sensing it, witnessing it. The witness is you; the fear is not.

Shortly, an interesting phenomenon will occur: the fear will disappear. Its disappearance will dispel any aggression that the snake might have felt towards you. It will also restore your presence of mind so that you can act appropriately. Furthermore, your shift of focus will exercise the spiritual muscle required to separate your higher self from your lower nature. That shift is the beginning of transformation, the birth of awareness that you are not your emotions.

3
Principles
of Truth

Colors:
Effects on the Body

Karsta came from Germany to marry an American medical student. She belonged to a small circle of seekers in Mannheim who adhered to singular practices: group meditations on new- and full-moon nights, eating only one meal a day at the noon hour, and wearing only light blue. Karsta seemed to be seeking validity for her practices.

"We believe that our environment needs healing," she began, "and that healing starts with the individual. Our teacher says that the color blue calms body and mind vibrations, for those who wear it and for those who see it. She said too that blue can heal people if they just look at it. Not many Germans or Americans understand this process. Can you share any knowledge about color?"

D. We Westerners tend to adopt a fact here and a fact there and piece them together out of context. This problem does not occur in the East because the outlook there is synthesistic; it starts out with a view of the Whole.

Like sounds, colors are potent energies with distinctive force fields and effects too subtle and complicated to address here. But I can share something about their effects through a true story about a woman who loved the color blue.

Growing up, this woman wore blue as often as she could. When she was in her twenties, virtually all her clothes were blue. On her first trip to India, she stayed in an ashram. Her room had no closet, so she hung all her garments on a cord strung from one side of the room to the other. When she got up in the morning, these clothes were the first things she saw.

One morning she opened her eyes, and this sea of blueness hit her in the stomach. She became violently ill. Inexplicable as this phenomenon was to her American background, she knew without any doubt that the uninterrupted mass of blue had caused the nausea. Unable to look at the color, she removed her garments from the string with her eyes closed, wrapped them up in a sheet, and gave them away. Someone gave her a white sari and a blouse. She never wore blue again.

Ayurveda, a system of medicine indigenous to India, can help explain some of the dynamics of this physical reaction. Every object in the universe consists of five elements: hardness (earth), liquidity (water), heat (fire), movement (air), and space (ether). In the human body, Ayurveda tells us, earth and water combine to form the humor called *kapha;* water and fire form *pitta;* air and ether form *vatta.* Every human constitution is dominated by one of these three humors. The humors govern our lives: our tendency to be fat or thin, our appetite, elimination, temperament, pulse, mode of sleep and dreams, speech, dryness and softness of our hair and skin. In *Ayurveda: The Science of Self-Healing, A Practical Guide,* Dr. Vasant Lad offers guidelines to help readers determine their constitutional type.

These humors govern how prone we are to particular diseases. For example, a kapha constitution is prone to tonsilitis, sinusitis, and bronchitis; pitta constitutions, to disorders of the gall bladder, liver and bile, ulcers, and hyperacidity; vatta constitutions are prone to gas, lower back pain, arthritis, sciatica, and neuralgia. Unlike Western doctors who prescribe one medical remedy for everybody with the same disease, Ayurvedic doctors first determine the constitution of a patient. A pitta-governed cancer patient receives different medication from a kapha cancer case.

So Ayurveda teaches that what is good for one person is not necessarily good for everyone. That applies to foods, herbs, medicines, gems, stones, and colors. These can either aggravate or regulate a body humor. Dr. Lad's book shows how to select these items for our individual constitution and health problems.

Let's get back to color. In the same way that heat characterizes the color red, coldness characterizes the color blue. Coldness is a characteristic of vatta and kapha. If kapha- or vatta-predominant persons wear blue exclusively, the color will affect them adversely. The woman I spoke about was troubled from childhood by kapha problems. The constant use of blue aggravated the kapha humor until her body reached a saturation point.

K. Could her reaction have been only temporary?
D. No.
K. How can you be sure of that?
D. The incident occurred twenty-five years ago, and there still isn't a shred of blue in my closet!

Death:
The Dance of Death
Wears the Mask of Life

Newlyweds Ken and Lola made a handsome couple. Lola meditated, prayed, and read scriptures daily. At her insistence, Ken came to the workshop. "I want our marriage to work," Lola told us. "I know it would if we could share the spiritual life." Ken objected. "She can do what she wants," he said, "but why must she insist that I join her? I had a hard time when I grew up. Now I want to enjoy myself. Later there will be plenty of time to think about spiritual things. Even in my sixties I'll have enough time left. Don't you think I'm justified?"

D. No one can tell you whether you are justified in not joining your wife. Your heart alone knows. But your decision should rest on fact, not fancy. I want to address your statement that your sixties will be time enough.

First of all, spiritual activity is not sealed off in a watertight compartment divorced from your world. Your spiritual dimension is your center, and it should constitute the center of all your activity. Your dynamism flows from that still center. The stronger the center is, the better will be your health, relationships, and work.

Second, consider what different teachers have said about the thought that we have plenty of time. In Carlos Castaneda's *Journey to Ixtlan*, teacher Don Juan tells Castaneda that death is our eternal companion. "It is always to your left," he says, "at an arm's length." He tries to get Castaneda to see it, but Castaneda does not want to think about death. It makes him uncomfortable. Don Juan tells him that he should not be like most people who live as though they were never going to die. "Death is the wisest advisor one has," he says.

The Buddha put the point another way. A man was walking through the woods when a tiger saw him and started to run after him. The man ran fast, but at the edge of the forest, he came to a deep precipice. A jump would kill him, but so would the tiger. He looked up and grabbed hold of a vine. Swinging in the air, he looked beneath him. There on a plateau was another tiger. Both tigers roared at him. He got even more scared when he saw two little mice nibbling at the vine that was keeping him alive. One mouse was black and one was white. Suddenly he spotted a little strawberry growing on the side of a cliff. He plucked it and ate it. Forgetting his real plight, he got distracted by the luscious taste of the strawberry. "How delicious!" he exclaimed. "I wish I could find another one!"

In the throes of delight, we forget how transitory are earthly joys. Days and nights (the two little mice) nibble nonstop at our lives. Whether we are handsome, ugly, rich, poor, smart, or dumb, we cannot escape the universal phenomenon of uncertainty. Like the tigers in the story, death always lurks around us, and not merely behind old age. Tigers lurk in unexpected sickness, accidents, and destruction by other humans, creatures, earthquakes, and storms. Not long ago, Baba Ram Dass, a spiritual teacher who does a lot of prison work, told Dr. Elisabeth Kübler-Ross how remarkable it is that so many people he lectured to were open to discussions about death. She remarked, "Well, don't you understand—we're all on death row."

In the *Imitation of Christ*, St. Thomas á Kempis writes that at any moment one can be swallowed up by the jaws of death: "When evening comes, venture not to promise thyself the next morning. Be always in readiness. Live that death may never find thee unprepared. For the Son of Man will come at the hour when He is not looked for....Provide now, in time."

So the issue lies not in whether you are justified in not sharing your wife's spiritual pursuits. The issue is that fact rather than fancy should determine your decisions. Never forget that the ubiquitous presence of death always wears the mask of life.

Disease:
Causes and Cures
from the Inside Out

Senior nurse Yvonne came to my workshop on "Eastern Secrets of Longevity and Health." "I was never interested in this sort of thing," she began, "until I saw a miracle happen in front of my eyes. A so-called 'terminal' cancer patient began to meditate on a perfect state of health, on 'seeing' and feeling his liver in perfect condition. He recovered, and astonished his doctors."

Yvonne read everything she could get on the body-mind relationship, including *Stress* by Hans Selye, *Anatomy of an Illness* by Norman Cousins, and the works of senior cancer researcher Dr. Carl Simonton. Then she began to meditate. "I can see the power in it," she said. "When my mind is quiet, it seems like a great blank sheet of paper. I can write what I want on it and I get the feeling that I am creating my destiny. What I don't understand is, am I not creating my destiny all day long, every day, even when I am not meditating?"

D. You are. We all are, but our haphazard flow of uncontrolled thought brings haphazard results. A blank mind is like a fertile field with no weeds to impede growth. A mind filled with random thoughts is like a field full of weeds.

Y. I would like to teach meditation to cancer patients, but not many are interested. I tell them about the "miraculous" recovery I saw, but very few take me seriously. Since people like Dr. Selye, Norman Cousins, and Dr. Simonton have written books and given testimonials to the effects of mind on body, why should there still be so much disbelief?

D. For several reasons. Working on our physical conditions with our minds needs no outside help and it costs us nothing. Here in the West we grow up to believe that if something is free it is worthless; if it carries a price tag, it has value. Second, we are taught to depend upon and respect our institutions—religious, educational, and medical. They validate our experience and give us guidance.

Medical schools do not teach their students about spiritual dynamics, the effects of meditation and thoughts on the body, the existence of the subtle body, the nadis or nerve channels that link mind to the chakras—centers of psychic energy linked to the glands or the body humors. So Western doctors ignore all the evidence because it does not fit into their frame of reference. After all, medical school costs them a lot of money.

New knowledge has punctured our frames of reference in all disciplines—physics, medicine, education, religion, ecology. Yet we are scared to accept it, scared that we cannot cope with the discrepancy between our experience and our bag of outmoded concepts. Like people who are walking up a second staircase and clinging to the banister of the first one, we won't let go.

Here is an example of what I mean. For sixteen years a woman suffers with terrible asthma. American doctors relieve her attacks with adrenalin and cortisone. They cost a lot, and they have dreadful side effects.

184

A New York specialist tells her with total certitude that asthma is, has been, and always will be incurable. Off she goes to India. She pays two rupees for a diagnosis and medicine to a doctor of Ayurveda, a 5000-year-old medical system that addresses the whole person. Two days later, all asthmatic attacks stop and never come back. When she returns to the United States, she tells the New York doctor. He laughs. What else can he do? Her experience lies outside of his frame of reference. This story is not fiction. *It happened to me.*

Here is another true example. Doctors tell Jane that if she does not have surgery to remove her brain tumor, she won't live longer than three months. Jane doesn't want surgery. For twenty-one days nonstop, she repeats a sacred healing mantra that goes on even in her sleep. On the next X-ray, not a trace of the tumor is left. The X-rays make the point. But the point does not fit the establishment's frame of reference. The doctors call it a hoax, put it out of mind, and get on with the old show.

Colleagues thought Einstein was eccentric when he said that he did not arrive at his understanding of the fundamental laws of the universe through his rational mind. In *Grist For The Mill,* Baba Ram Dass called the rational mind "the high priest of our society." He writes, "I remember as a social scientist I studied what was studiable. What was studiable had nothing to do with what was happening to me, but it was studiable."

Decades ago, Dr. Troskin, a Russian cancer specialist, showed how the white blood cell count of his terminal cancer cases plummeted with every input of a negative word, and rose just as high with every positive input. Renowned cancer researcher, British General Surgeon Dr. Douglas Stevenson, said many years ago: "The supreme irony is that the essential evidence [the cause and cure] is man himself." Yet how many professionals

185

look at *the person* with an eye to habits of mind, and physical habits like diet as the cause and cure of illness? There is no money in it. Surely, doctors think, a cure will be discovered only when another billion dollars is poured into more areas where researchers can look for the culprit.

Y. Is there some way that I could present this to my patients—an easy nontechnical, nonabstract explanation they could relate to?

D. You might start off by telling them that everything in the universe happens from the inside out. Nothing ever happens from the outside in. The tail never wags the dog.

Freedom:
God is Boundless Freedom

Alan, a civil engineer in his fifties, takes daily meditation as seriously as he does his Catholic tradition. Every morning for the last twenty years, he has meditated in his study from 5:00 to 6:30 A.M. This, he says, is the best part of his day.

"It frees me from feeling limited," he told us. "Freedom is what I want. It is what I have always wanted. In my younger days, I looked for it everywhere. I rebelled against institutions and regulations that I thought imprisoned me. Not until I was thirty-five did I realize that both the prisons and the freedom were inside of me.

"A couple of weeks ago, I had a long talk with my pastor. He said that I was on the wrong track and that seeking freedom was selfish. But to me, freedom is God. What is your opinion?"

D. Many years ago I took flying lessons in a Piper cub at a small airfield outside of Chicago. For my first eight hours of instruction when I sat behind my instructor, I felt no thrill. But then I was ready for my solo flight. A brilliant sun shone on that morning. The wind sock barely moved. As I pulled the stick back and the nose of the plane shot up towards the sky, I thought,

"My God! *This is freedom!*" In front of me, above, behind, right and left was an infinite expanse of boundless space.

Then I came down, literally and figuratively. My instructor blasted me for making a bumpy three-point landing. An hour later, I was driving back to Chicago in the midst of heavy traffic, blasting a truck driver who nearly sideswiped me. What happend to the bliss, I wondered. Where did it go? I thought there ought to be a way to bottle that freedom and imbibe it anywhere.

Twelve years later, after I was initiated into the world of inner experience, I sat on the banks of the Ganges surrounded by the Himalayan foothills. For forty-five minutes I had been meditating. With my eyes closed and my mind finally free of thought, my consciousness suddenly soared above my body. Below, beyond, behind, above, right, and left was a limitless expanse of space. I was catapulted into that expanse and I became it! Unlike the day of my solo flight when there was space and me, on this flight space and I became one. Here was freedom beyond the grasp of the mind. It infused me with a peace that transformed my life.

In my experience, God is boundless freedom; and boundless freedom is God.

God:
God Is One but Names Are Many

Anna taught Hatha Yoga and meditation for many years at a midcity yoga center. "I'd like to include chanting in our meditation sessions," she said, "but Americans have problems with all these names of God. Is there an easy way to explain this dimension of Indian philosophy?"

D. In the West, God has only one name. In the East, God has many names, but that does not mean that there are many gods. God is only one. Names are adjectives that represent functions of God's power of expression. Ganesh, for example, signifies the function of removing obstacles. Depicted as elephant-headed, the energy of Ganesh is like an elephant clearing a path through a forest. On its own plane of existence, Ganesh does not have an elephant head; the imagery is ours to give us a hook on which to hang our thoughts. Prayers to Ganesh are prayers to the Divine in its form as obstacle-remover, and not to a separate God.

A. Why is it necessary to pray to Ganesh? Why can't we simply pray to God?

D. Innumerble powers and functions are required for the process of creating, sustaining, and dissolving our universes. Have you ever seen detailed charts of

189

the divisions of functions within large organizations? Infinitely more complicated than organizations is a universe. It contains many worlds, many planes of existence, and many kinds of beings.

A. What are some of the functions of powers whose names are used commonly in chanting?

D. Wisdom, knowledge, opulence, love, victory, will, grace, harmony, fearlessness, protection.

A. Do we imbibe those energies or powers when we chant or pray to them?

D. That is the purpose of it. Through chanting names of God, or repeating mantras or through worship, we open ourselves as a channel of that energy. We become what we meditate on.

A. If we are that one absolute Reality, why can't we just worship ourselves?

D. We do worship ourselves, but not the right way. Look how we worship our bodies. We decorate them with lavish clothing, jewelry, perfumes, and creams. We feed them richly. We lay them on beds with soft mattresses. If we regarded all these actions as an offering to God and saw our bodies as the form of God, our body worship would become an effective spiritual practice.

A. When we repeat the various names of these powers of God, when we chant or worship them, do we get palpable, concrete help from them? Or is it all abstract?

D. Recently I read of a woman with no formal education who can multiply two thirteen-digit numbers in less than thirty seconds, and she does it correctly. She could not explain her genius in any way other than to say that when she needs knowledge, she turns to Ganesh. She even beat one of the fastest computers in finding the twenty-third root of a two-hundred-and-one digit number. I would call that concrete and palpable. It made me think of an adage I heard some years ago: ''If religion is the opium of the people, India has the inside dope.''

God:
Impersonal and
Personal—Be-er and Do-er

A native of Detroit, Jim lectured on love and healing to executives and salesmen in the automobile industry. He read books on Theosophy, Taoism, Vedanta, yoga, and Buddhism. He attended workshops to deepen his understanding and incorporate it into his work.

"In Christianity, one hears only about the personal God," he said. "Taoism and Vedanta focus only on the impersonal. That dichotomy confuses me. Are there two different 'Gods'? If so, how do they relate to each other? Or are they merely concepts?"

D. The personal and impersonal are not two different Gods nor are they concepts. They are two sides of the same coin. The nameless Truth has manifested itself as the entire universe, so every form you see, hear, touch, taste, smell, and think about is God. God's cosmic body is the totality of all bodies within it; God's mind is the aggregate of all minds. Just as there are billions of cells in your body, your body-mind complex is one of billions of "cells" in the personal or dynamic aspect of God. He or she, whichever word you choose, moves, thinks, animates, creates, sustains, and dissolves universes. This personal aspect is God's expression, power or energy.

Sri Ramakrishna, who is often described as the consummation of the spiritual life, makes this point clear in *The Gospel of Sri Ramakrishna* and *The Life of Sri Ramakrishna*. I have read his life twelve times and I am still reading it because it stirs my heart and stirs my mind. His works are filled with his experiences of both aspects of the Divine, the Mother (personal) and Brahman (impersonal).

Please also read a book written by a Westerner for Westerners: *Grist For The Mill* by Baba Ram Dass. Just as in the Tantric tradition of Sri Ramakrishna, Ram Dass refers to the personal aspect of God as the Mother: ''The entire universe, all of its forms, all form is the Mother. You are all part of the Mother. The Mother has many faces. . . . Some are wrathful, some are tender. . . . For me, the Mother covers the world. . . .

''I cover the world with the Mother. . . . through my daily life situations. . . . My body is part of the Mother. I feed on the Mother. I absorb the Mother. I drink the Mother. I feed at the breast of the Mother continuously. The Mother is the shakti, the juice, the vibration, the energy of the universe. I keep growing inside as I feed more and more. I have to consume the Mother . . . . I consume the violence, the beauty. . . . I am consuming the Mother and I am taking all that energy and using it in order to stay with God.''

In contrast to this dynamism of the personal aspect, the impersonal pure Awareness is still and silent. This is the Reality, the ground and substratum of our being—existence, consciousness, and bliss. It is all-pervading light, partless, changeless, nameless, formless, and indivisible. This is the Brahman which comes from the Sanskrit word *Briha* meaning ''all'' or ''infinite.'' Brahman is like the number one before a string of zeroes. Take away the one and the zeroes come to nothing. When all forms subside, only the impersonal Reality remains.

J. I don't understand the relationship between the personal and impersonal.

D. Think of a statue and a block of stone: statue is personal; stone is impersonal. Stone is the stuff that constitutes the statue. Or think of a gold earring: the earring, a function, is personal; gold is impersonal, the stuff of which the ornament is made. Stated another way, the impersonal is the be-er. The personal is the do-er.

J. Where do I come in?

D. You *are* it. Jim with his memories, desires, likes, dislikes, talents, personality, body, and mind is a microcosmic unit in the macrocosmic body of the personal. Your real identity is impersonal Awareness—pure being-consciousness-bliss. You are unattached, cosmic, silent, and eternal. No calamity or torture, nothing that Jim does or thinks, can affect that.

J. If my body-mind complex is a part of the personal aspect of God, and if my Awareness is also cosmic, then what is left? Who am I? Or what is "I"?

D. That is the cosmic joke—the illusion, the myth, Maya. There isn't any "I." To realize this is the reason we read books and meditate, why we take birth after birth, in form after form. We are like a cup filled with ocean water that floats on the surface of the sea. The cup thinks that it is totally individual. That thought itself creates the contours of the cup. The more entrenched the "I" thought, the denser and more impermeable are its contours.

J. How do you get out of that bind?

D. Spiritual practice thins out the "I." Practice makes the cup porous. One day the cup becomes so porous that it dissolves, and the water within merges with the water without. There was never any difference between them; but when that knowledge becomes experience, the wheel of birth and death comes to a halt. At long last, we have come home.

God:
To a Little Frog,
God Is a Big Frog

Values such as selfless service, compassion, and integrity governed Florence's life. She was only in her junior year at a midwestern college, yet for several years, she had volunteered her weekends at a drug abuse clinic. She sensed the presence of a higher Force, but she could not identify herself with any path.

"It bothers me," she told us, "that there are so many paths, so many religions, so many churches. Why must it be this way? Why can't Truth be known as Truth, clear and simple?"

D. We hear that man is made in the image of God, but the converse is also true. God is conceived in the image of man. Because our minds differ, our concepts of Truth differ. Of course our conceptions can never limit that Supreme Majesty. Our conceptions limit only our experience of it.

F. But I don't understand why we can't see that Absolute Truth as it is.

D. Most of us live in an ordinary mental consciousness in which we cannot experience the highest Truth directly. All we can do is conceptualize. Mind is the highest faculty that most of us know. So we use it to think about God like we think about an apple. Mind is finite; an apple is finite. Thinking about an apple is no problem for the mind. But how can a finite vehicle perceive what lies beyond it? It can't. Mind must be stilled so that the Absolute can know itself.

F. Is there any path on which people see the Absolute as it really is?

D. The path is not the issue. The issue is the process. Seekers on any and every path who rise beyond the mind can see Truth as it is because spirit or Consciousness is the vehicle of their experience. Consciousness underlies everything in the universe. Descriptions of the experience may vary according to one's vocabulary, culture, and tradition. But the experience of the highest Truth is always the same.

F. Then there is no way for ordinary people to have that same experience?

D. Like the sun that shines on everyone without discrimination, truth is accessible to the ordinary as well as to the extraordinary when they transcend their minds. Even a rogue can know God if he rises beyond mind. Once he does, transformation occurs. Until we go beyond thought, God or Truth is projected through our "psychic grid."

In *The Psychic Grid,* Dr. Beatrice Bruteau explains lucidly the process by which we create our realities. She writes that these grids determine our perceptions and conceptions. "They are not *what* we experience. They are frameworks in the senses and in the mind itself *by which* we experience. . . . There is no such thing as 'raw' experience, experience that is unfiltered, unsorted, unevaluated. What registers within as actual conscious experience is always the product of both the incoming *stimulus* and the *significance* we attach to it by the operation of our psychic grid." To grow, Dr. Bruteau tells us, we have to learn to tune the grid "in the sense of refining a chosen grid to obtain the elaboration and subtlety we desire, and in the sense of shifting to 'another station,' another grid entirely."

I heard an Indian sage say that the entire universe is a projection of our minds. A young man from Germany asked him, "Does a little frog also project a mental picture of the universe?"

"Certainly."

"Can a frog have a sense of God's existence?" asked the seeker.

"Everything in the universe has that sense," the sage replied. "Every creature, no matter how lowly, even an atom, has a built-in yearning to return to its center, to its Source."

"How would a little frog think of God?" the student asked.

"To a little frog," said the sage, "God would be a great big frog."

Holiness:
His Holiness—His Hollowness

Chris, a former priest from Virginia who had become a counsellor, sought light on the Eastern perspective of holiness. ''The term 'holiness' is not used as much in the West as it is in the East,'' Chris said. ''To me, real holiness is virtually impossible to achieve in the times we're living in. The best we can do is to try to follow Christ. We can lag far behind him, but at least we should stay on his road instead of going the opposite way. To my mind, following Jesus is all that seems possible. So I don't understand how the 'holy man' idea can be used so commonly in the East.''

D. The difference in perspective is fundamental. The Christian perspective is that we are all born as sinners. The state of holiness is foreign to us. Such a foreign state would not be merely hard to attain; it would be impossible. The Eastern perspective is that divinity is inherent in all creation. So the state of holiness is accessible to all who work on removing the dross that obscures it.

In Hindu mythology, the Lord is often depicted as a flute player. When you play a wind instrument, you know that the apertures must be kept absolutely clean for the sound to come through clearly. Similarly, the purer we are or the emptier we are of the notions of individuality, do-ership, ego, concepts, ideas, and opinions, the less the Divine expression will be impeded. This truth is implied in St. Paul's statement, "Not I doeth anymore, but Christ doeth within me."

In India, the term "holiness" refers to men and women in whom all sense of "I" and "mine" has dissolved. "His Holiness" really means "His Hollowness."

Inclusivity:
Criterion for a Valid Teaching

Beverly, a mother of three teenagers, worked as a librarian in a large city. For many years she had done "spiritual window shopping." She went to every spiritual workshop, lecture, and retreat that she could, and she tried many mantras, meditations, and gurus.

"At this point I'm confused," Beverly said. "What I'm looking for is a genuine path. I don't want to get hooked into a setup as part of a herd of sheep that a commercial pied piper is wooing. I came here to ask you how spiritual seekers can discriminate. How do you know when a teaching is genuine? I need down-to-earth criteria."

D. When you say "genuine," what do you mean?
B. I mean teaching that will take me to truth, not one that will stuff somebody's pockets or make his name a household word. I want God-Realization, unity consciousness. I want to know that we are all one, not intellectually but in experience. Are there criteria I can use to judge whether I am on the right track?
D. When I was learning how to fly a Piper cub, I had to practice three-point landings. To make a perfect three-point landing, the plane must get into the three-point posture just before it touches ground. If its angle

is off, the landing is off. I have found that practicing the "posture" of what we want to attain also applies to almost everything else we wish to have or to become.

An Indian master said that for union with God we must become like God. So we have to clarify our understanding of God. Surely, God must personify every virtue we can imagine: love, mercy, wisdom, beauty, purity, perfection. Would God shun or favor a color, creed, hemisphere, or people who worshipped only one Divine name and not others? Or would God regard all differences as manifestations of Divinity?

The cosmic perspective would be as limitless as infinity, for all creation is God's form. A genuine teaching should reflect that perspective. It should be a circle whose center is everywhere and whose circumference is nowhere.

B. Many groups claim that kind of teaching and brotherhood.

D. Quite so. To know whether their claims are valid, we need to open our eyes. Often their term "brotherhood" refers only to the "brothers" under their own hood. A genuine teaching never posits that there is only one way, one name, one guru. It turns our eyes towards the canvas on which the figures are painted. Looking at the canvas, we see differences but not separation.

B. How do I find a path that focuses on the canvas, on our unity?

D. The path will find you. Your Sadguru within has already made your goal clear. Trust that it will attract the right path to you. As Ram Dass put it in *Grist For The Mill*, "You will start to fall into a lineage, not because it's the hip thing to do...but because that way pulled you. A lineage...in which the teacher is a free being is one that catapults you ultimately out the other end; it isn't designed to make you a follower of the lineage, it is designed to take you through itself and free you at the other end. A less pure teaching of a lineage traps you."

B. How can I tell that I'm not getting trapped?

D. By noting whether you see more or fewer differences in people. The sign of progress is a gradual shift of inner focus from the figures to the canvas— seeing more of the backdrop and less of the play. Backdrop is unity. Play is diversity. You get to a place that contains both and goes beyond them.

Let me put this another way. When you read through books at your library, you focus on the print. As you follow a path and take up its practices, see if your focus changes from the printed words of life to the space on which they are printed—from changing forms to changeless space beyond. If your mind hangs onto the ink, you may be walking on the wrong path. If your perception moves to the space, you're headed towards unity.

Like the canvas, the space provides us with the criterion for a valid spiritual teaching. We can sum it up in one word—*inclusivity*.

Indwelling Lord:
In Saints and Sinners

Budapest-born Tibor lives in a small town in the south where he practices dentistry and teaches yoga in his waiting room to children of preschool and school age. Every evening he and his wife and two sons do Hatha Yoga, meditate, and read together from the *Bhagavad Gita*.

"On Sundays we go to a Catholic church where I lead short meditations and talk about spiritual growth. Most important to me is the Vedanta philosophy of One becoming many. If we can't understand that, then we can't see the indwelling Lord in all. And seeing that is our key to survival.

"Last week I told them about the *Bhagavad Gita*, about how Arjuna, a warrior, refuses to fight a battle because he sees his teachers, family, and friends on the enemy lines. He can see them all—their heads and eyes and ears and arms and legs—and he would rather be killed than kill them.

"Then I read to the congregation a part of the chapter where Sri Krishna bestows the vision of his cosmic form on Arjuna. Suddenly the warrior sees that these heads and arms and legs belong not to separate people but to the body of God. So the whole battlefield is no longer a scene of one army fighting another, but the Lord expressing himself in myriads of roles.

"The congregation enjoyed the talk. But many couldn't accept it. They said, 'It's impossible to see God in everyone, especially in a sinner.' Can you show me how to help them realize that the Lord dwells in everybody, saint and sinner alike?"

D. To perceive God in all forms is not easy. Such a vision does not come from merely hearing others talk about it. Seers of all traditions who have risen to the top of this mount got there the hard way: tough, protracted spiritual disciplines and intense devotion to the Truth—one-pointed devotion. The climb is steep, and there are no shortcuts.

You can, however, incline others' minds and hearts in that direction. For your congregation, you might quote the experiences of a fellow Catholic, the late Trappist monk Thomas Merton. After a profound inner experience of God, Merton went out into the town outside his Kentucky monastery and was stunned: Everything was God! Not merely people, but also dogs and pillars and concrete.

The Early Fathers of the Desert had similar experiences. You can quote them from *The Philokalia*. Instructions they give to attain high states of consciousness differ very little from the instructions of Eastern sages. I recall in particular one passage from a second century Philokalian text: "He who does not limit his perception of the nature of visible things *to what his senses alone can observe,* but wisely with his intellect searches after the Essence which lies within every creature, also finds God." The Father counsels that every Christian who seeks Christ should discriminate between Essence and outward appearance. He doesn't say, "Discriminate between Essence and saintly appearance."

Here is a true story that your friends might relate to because it occurred in our own culture. Several years ago in the auditorium of a large ashram in New York State, thousands of Americans visited Baba Muktananda daily. One evening, Baba was talking about the Self as the indivisible Reality behind everything in the universe. After his talk, as was the custom, visitors walked down the aisle in a long queue, presented him with flowers or fruit, and asked a question if they wished. On this occasion, a young woman who was dressed somewhat inappropriately placed her flower in front of him, and said, "If you knew what I am, you would not take that flower."

"Who are you?" Baba asked.

The young woman looked up and dared to say it. "I am a prostitute."

For a full minute, Baba fixed his eyes on hers. Around him nearly a thousand Americans sat, still as statues, holding their breath.

"When I look at you," Baba said, "I do not see a prostitute. I see only the Self!"

Liberation:
A Portrait

Tatiana taught Russian in Washington, D.C., where a noon-time yoga club awakened her interest in the spiritual life. She read spiritual books ''greedily,'' she said. ''What troubles me is that it takes too much time to realize the Self. Too many things to do and not to do. I thought of a shortcut. The idea comes from my childhood.''

When Tatiana was eight years old, her mother told her she had a weak personality, ''like the Russian equivalent of an American jellyfish.'' Her parents accused her of hunching her back, being too shy to raise her head, and speaking too softly for others to hear. In contrast, her twelve-year-old brother was tall, confident, and forceful. ''Nobody told me how to change,'' she said, ''but I was so jealous of Pyotr that I watched him secretly and made notes. Head up, lips pursed, hands on hips, bellow out words, and so on. Then I would practice. To my parents' astonishment, within four months I struck everybody as the most confident child in our neighborhood.

''What I have in mind now is to study the behavior of liberated people and practice it. The principle should work the same way. You have been close to sages and masters, so I thought you could give me a word portrait of a Self-realized person."

D. The problem is that, unlike a confident person, a liberated person wears no signs, nor do any two liberated people act alike. Here are a few word portraits from the *Narada Bhakti Sutras* (published by the Sri Ramakrishna Math in Madras).

"The conduct and behaviour of the perfected soul are sometimes as inscrutable as the ways of the Lord Himself. No man can predict what he may or may not do. He has no will of his own, as he has already surrendered it completely to the Lord. He is not the slave of so-called common sense or reason. . .nor is he in the grip of conventional laws of society or scriptures. He is under the benign influence of a higher Power than human, and his behaviour and conduct depend upon how this higher Power makes use of him for Its own inscrutable purposes. His conduct, being sometimes strange, and at other times unintelligible from the standpoint of ordinary human reason and experience, may often appear similar to those of lunatics though his behaviour can never go against Dharma."

In *The Gospel of Sri Ramakrishna* (published by the Ramakrishna-Vivekananda Center), the master states that when a man attains the knowledge of Brahman, he may act like a five-year-old child, a madman, or an inert thing.

Papa Ramdas, the Indian sage of Kerala, writes in *God-Experience* that the only external sign of realized beings is that they attract people like magnets. All other signs are known only to themselves. They are conscious that they are immortal and not subject to birth, growth, decay, and death. They have no fear because they know that they are not the body but the immortal Spirit. The sense of sin is absent in them; they are free from ideas of sin and virtue, good and evil, birth and death. Their bliss is constant.

Self-Knowledge by Adi Shankaracharya reiterates that the bliss of the liberated one is constant. "Though he may sometimes seem to others to be like an unillumined person. . .he himself is never oblivious of his real nature of Immortal Consciousness. . . .He does not dwell on the enjoyments of the past, takes no thought of the future, and is indifferent about the present. . . .

"Though a liberated being lives in a world of diversity, he is unruffled by the pairs of opposites. Whether tormented by the wicked or worshipped by the good, he remains undisturbed. [He] transcends the scriptures and social conventions. He is beyond the imperatives of ethics. Yet he cannot do anything that is not good and not conducive to the welfare of others. . . .

"He may wear no outer mark of holiness. Free from desires, he enjoys material objects but never forgets his omnipotent Divine Self. . . .

"Though without riches, yet ever content; though helpless, yet endowed with exceeding power; though detached from sense objects, yet eternally satisfied; he neither directs the senses to their objects nor detaches them from these, but looks on as an unconcerned spectator, and he has not the least craving for the fruits of action, his mind being thoroughly intoxicated with drinking the undiluted elixir of the Bliss of Atman."

In *I Am That* Sri Nisargadatta says that there are no distinctive marks of jnana. Only ignorance can be recognized, not jnana.

The masters I have known differ from one another as much as all the rest of us do. One has an atrocious, merciless personality, which has the effect of weeding out the weak. He is a tiger on the outside and a dove on the inside. Yet, another master in the same lineage is a dove on the outside and a tiger within. Both have extraordinary powers, yet rarely use them. Neither claims to be anything special but both are like magnets. All this shows you how hard it is to emulate outer behavior in order to arrive at a high inner state. But perhaps this advice might help you.

A Western seeker told Sri Nisargadatta that, despite his inspiring words, she felt limited. "What am I to do?" she asked the sage. "I do not see myself as you see me. Maybe you are right and I am wrong, but how can I cease to be what I feel I am?"

Sri Nisargadatta replied: "A prince who believes himself to be a beggar can be convinced conclusively in one way only: he must behave as a prince and see what happens. Behave as if what I say is true and judge by what actually happens. . . .

"Behave as if you were pure awareness, bodiless and mindless, spaceless and timeless, beyond 'where' and 'when' and 'how.' Dwell on it, think of it, learn to accept its reality. . . . Make your mind and body express the real which is all and beyond all. By doing, you succeed."

The seeker he spoke to had been on the spiritual path for a long, long time. But perhaps his advice can work for newcomers too. Try it. Look at Sri Nisargadatta's words as you looked at Pyotr. Be clear about it. Be constant about it. Be intense about it. Make written and mental notes: "I am pure awareness. I am not this body. I am not this mind. I exist beyond space and time. I AM THAT. Stick to this method until you reach the goal. You may be right. This route may be the shortest cut from beggar to prince and the hottest line to liberation.

Liberation:
Everybody Wants It

Donald, a soft-spoken college student, sought to know why more people did not pursue liberation. "If just a little spiritual experience gives so much bliss, then Cosmic Consciousness must surely be ecstasy. If that's the case," he asked, "why do so few people go for it?"

D. Everybody wants liberation. Every creature in the universe wants to be free, happy, and live forever. Most people seek this freedom and joy in food, sex, money, travel, name, fame, and entertainment. The problem is not that people don't want liberation, but that they look for it in the wrong places.

Easterners depict this situation in the story of a village woman who was digging through a stack of hay outside her hut. A man came along on a donkey and asked, "What are you looking for?"

"A needle," she said.

"Where did you drop it?"

The woman turned and pointed to her hut. "In there."

"Then why are you looking for it outside?" he asked.

"Oh!" she said, "it's much too dark in there!"

All that we seek lies within. The Seeker is the sought. As Jesus said, the Kingdom of Heaven is within. Paradoxically, that all-pervading Light hides itself beneath a cloud of unknowing. When meditation and sense-withdrawal dispel the cloud, the Self experiences itself.

Most of us are like a mother monkey hunting everywhere for her baby while the baby is sitting on her back.

New Physics:
The Quantum Leap into Life

When Ivar, a university art student, visited his uncle in Norway, he learned about metaphysics for the first time. "I got interested," he told us, "because I saw it as a way to access truth. I would like to share it with colleagues in my commune. The problem is that most of them study physics or medicine. What links between metaphysics and physics can I show them? How does metaphysics validate physics?"

D. It seems to me that it is the other way around. Physics validates metaphysics. Some years ago physics took the quantum leap. Quantum physics did not leap into tomorrow; it leapt into the timeless reality of every mystic. It jumped from "separate, independent subject versus separate, independent object" into one inseparable and boundless network of interconnected processes. That was the great truth, the great link. But for the sake of convenience, and in laymen's terms, let's look at the leap in three different ways to see three basic links.

First, quantum physics revealed that a subatomic particle such as an electron could no longer be defined as a static substance or by what it *is*. It can be described only in terms of what it *does*, in other words, by its patterns of behavior within a complex web of interconnections and interactions. A metaphysical view, in keeping with Eastern teachings, says that the universe is Consciousness in action. Forms are energy, dynamic patterns of energy vibrating at varying rates of velocity. Like an electron, a human being *is* a function rather than *has* a function.

Second, a subatomic particle can no longer be isolated as an independent existence or process. It is now understood to be a part of an indivisible unity. The metaphysical view I mentioned reveals the unifying Ground of Being on which this cosmic web is woven. This Reality—through its inherent power of expression—is the ultimate agency of action. We are not autonomous. We are not separate beings contained in bags of skin.

I. Why do we appear separate?

D. Space gets in the way. Yet, space is an integral part of the process I mentioned. The space around us lies within us, just as the space in a cup is the same as the space outside it. Our illusion is our false identification with the shape of the cup or the contour we call our body. We are Consciousness, one Ground of Being in which all cups, bodies, and forms interact.

A third aspect of the quantum leap is that even the act of observing alters the observed. In current experiments, the observer is now considered a *participator*. Quantum physics merged observer and field. Similarly, Eastern philosophy speaks of how the one Universal Mind appears as both subject and object, just as in a dream state the individual mind divides itself into subject and object.

I. Where do you think physics will go from here?

D. Sooner or later physics has to ask the obvious question: If the observer of an experiment is a participator, then who is the *real* observer? Who observes both the participator and the field? If everything in the universe is dynamic and in a state of perpetual motion, surely there must be a static consciousness to perceive that motion. Only the static can perceive the dynamic. Only changelessness can perceive change. Science will ultimately come to "non-matter," Consciousness, the Ground of Being.

I. Why does it take so long for people to grasp such obvious truths?

D. The belief lag, I call it. Long ago people thought that the Earth was the center of the universe and that the sun revolved around it. Along came Copernicus who proved that the Earth revolved around the sun. His facts shook the world of science, but still they did not change anybody's life—that is, not until somebody woke up to the commercial potential. Copernicus' discovery, they figured, could help people cross the ocean and bring back the booty.

An hourglass symbolizes a lot to me—in this case, the link between physics and metaphysics. I see physics at the lower part of the hourglass with its broad base and diverse search for truth. Metaphysics is the top part that leads out to Source, with its infinite, synthesistic embrace. The quantum leap is the middle point where the physics of today meets the metaphysics of eternity. For thousands of years there have been metaphysicians who have posited that one Supreme Consciousness and its energy is all there is. The Dancer and its dance. Shiva and Shakti. Static and dynamic. Substance and pattern. Awareness and process. Knower and field.

I. What difference could it make to the world if people would accept these unseen universal laws?

D. Let's say quantum physics opened a church and called itself "The New Religion." The church would be like the middle point of the hourglass, a meeting point of physics and metaphysics, science and philosophy, today and eternity. Nobody would preach. Leaders in "spiritual physics" would teach the implications of the quantum leap. The leap itself would reveal the truth that the violent use of technology is like strangling our own throats with our own hands. With that revelation, we could take the quantum leap into life.

Occult Powers:
Strait is the Gate

As a child, Dudley often talked of God. He wanted to meet God, he would tell his folks. After high school, he tried to enter a cloistered monastic order. When they turned him down, he moved into a self-sustaining spiritual commune where residents meditated, maintained an organic garden, studied yoga, Tai Chi, I-Ching, Tarot, and martial arts. After meditating for three years, Dudley became clairvoyant.

"I got very excited," he said. "It was so uncanny. I could 'see' the person I was talking to on the telephone, the clothes they wore, their posture, everything. It knocked them out! Now I can see people in other parts of our house. How can I develop these powers and acquire others, like telepathy and psychokinesis?"

D. A disciple asked the Buddha the same question. He replied: "Precisely because I know what these powers do to people, I advise you to let them go instantly. Nothing can bring about the fall of a spiritual man faster than occult powers."

Dudley. I don't understand why occult powers are bad.

D. The Buddha did not say they are bad. He referred to what the powers *do* to people. Look at what often happens to the egos of people who wield political, economic, or social power. Occult powers carry much more danger than that.

Dudley. How can these powers cause me to fall when I've made so much progress already?

D. Spiritual teachers say that the higher you climb on the spiritual ladder, the more vulnerable you become. At higher altitudes, temptations are subtler. Besides, the higher the climb, the greater the fall.

Dudley. Why should I fall?

D. Look into your heart. Has your newly acquired clairvoyance turned your attention towards or away from your desire for God?

Dudley. I hadn't given it any thought. Perhaps it has turned my attention away temporarily, but I don't see why it should. Aren't occult powers a sign of spiritual progress?

D. On a few yogic paths they develop, but not on many. But even on those paths, a sign of progress is just a sign. It should never become a goal.

Dudley. Don't all spiritual masters have occult powers?

D. Some years ago Dr. Stanley Krippner, a highly esteemed researcher, author, and lecturer on parapsychology, told me that he knew spiritual masters who had no occult powers at all. On the other hand, he knew many people who manifest occult phenomena yet had no interest or development whatsoever in spirituality.

Dudley. But I am a spiritual man. Isn't the spiritual life like climbing a mountain? You don't climb vertically. You climb zig-zag. Perhaps this is a small detour that will help me on the spiritual path.

217

D. This story might explain the point. Once upon a time in ancient India, there was a Self-realized king who ruled over a vast kingdom. One day, he offered a reward for anyone who would carry a large vessel of water from the Ganges River to the main door of the palace without stopping for anything. "Remember!" the king shouted over a speaker on the morning of the contest. "No stopping! No stopping! No stopping!"

A thousand men turned up at the riverbank and started out together. When they had gone a furlong, they were surprised to see a gathering of beautiful women, half-nude, laughing and dancing around them. Two hundred men dropped out of the contest. Further on, the contestants spotted gold coins strewn all over the field. Another two hundred men dropped out to scoop them up. Still further ahead, the six hundred men saw a magnificent goddess of power dangling a set of keys. "Here they are," she said laughingly, "keys to the kingdom. The kingdom and the power is yours, whoever among you wants to rule the world." Two hundred men dropped their water bowls and ran for the keys.

Still further on the path, the remaining four hundred men saw another goddess. Breathtakingly beautiful and majestic, she stood behind a huge table of offerings. The offerings were occult powers. "Take what you want," she said. The table held the eight great *siddhis* or yogic powers, such as the power to make oneself invisible, to replicate oneself in other parts of the world, to make oneself tinier than a crystal or bigger than a tree, to fly through the air. All but one man succumbed.

When this lone contestant returned to the palace, the king asked him, "What did your eyes behold?"

"Only your face, revered King."

"What did your ears hear?" the king asked.

"Only your words, revered King: 'No stopping, no stopping, no stopping.' "

His grand prize was the key to the real Kingdom.

Wide is the gate and broad is the way that leadeth to destruction, and many there be which go in thereat: But strait is the gate, and narrow is the way which leadeth unto Life, and few there be that find it.

So said the Christ.

Peace:
Find the Common
Denominator

Hans came to my workshop on "Peace and the Spiritual Way." He worked for a peace organization that settled disputes between individuals and groups. "We work with people everywhere, from corporate boards and committees that are locked in conflict to senior citizens' centers. We achieve a fair measure of success. At times, though, we seem to go around in circles and just bandage the wounds. I came today to see whether I can find some spiritual peace tools that I can secularize without getting accused of being 'kooky.'"

D. The spiritual is not divorced from the secular. It is its still center like the sun and its rays. Spiritual and secular, inner and outer, seem like two yet they are one. But you are right. One should start gently. It is easier to bring people from the known to the unknown than the converse. How do you generally begin your peace workshops?

H. Our openers vary according to the situation. Last week we went to a senior citizens' center. We were all introduced to one another, and we told a few stories that got people laughing. Then two noninvolved members related a problem that had occurred between Group A and Group B. After that, representative speakers of each group told their side of the story, and we got on with our usual routine to help people see problems from the opposition's viewpoint.

D. I like the way you start. Laughter relaxes people. Let me share a few ideas that I use in conflict resolution workshops. Perhaps you can find something useful in them.

It seems to me that any collective unit—committee, club, organization, city, or country—is the collective consciousness made up of every individual consciousness in it. Like a necklace, it is the sum of its links or units. When every link is at peace, the necklace is peaceful. To have peace in the world or in any unit, we have to start with each individual heart.

One problem in resolving conflicts on the mental level is that mind is not the real conflict-solver. Mind is a conflict creator. Mind is the source of our ideas of separation, division, superiority, inferiority, preferences, judgments, and limitations. To solve conflicts we have to transcend the mind.

H. How can we transcend the mind in a mixed group situation? Some may be fundamentalists, some may be atheists, some may be farther along the path than I am.

D. I run into that situation all the time, but I do not consider it a problem. I try to treat it like fractions. When I went to school, we learned to add fractions by finding their common denominator.

H. We do the same. We try to find a common denominator.

D. Quite true, but I believe your common denominators lie on the mental level of ideas and attitudes. When I speak of a common denominator, however, I refer to the realm of Being, our only real common bond with others.

H. How do you develop that?

D. We don't have to. It comes with the package. We *are* it. Like the sun obscured by rain clouds, our common denominator gets eclipsed by our ideas of separation, superiority, and ego that trigger conflict. The closer people get to their common denominator, the less work a peace arbitrator has to do. At common denominator level, conflicts dissolve.

H. How do you approach that level?

D. You start with relaxation. People are uptight in conflicts. When they are uptight and their bodies and minds are tense, they can neither reach out to others nor receive an extended hand. To me, relaxation is the highest priority in all conflict situations. Through simple group exercises that can be done even on a hard chair, you can get people to relax. You can either lead the exercises yourself or use relaxation tapes available at most book stores.

H. What is the scientific value of the exercises?

D. The peace value is that when people are relaxed, they are more open. "Open" is a good word. Stretching your body feels good because it creates spaces. It doesn't really "create" space; it just gets the kinks out, and we feel more of the space that is already there. Similarly, when we relax our minds just enough to go beyond thought, space opens up. Stated more correctly, relaxation reduces the volume of our thoughts so that the space behind and between them becomes more apparent. When we feel more of our own space, we are open and we give more space to others. That openness is the launching pad for conflict resolution.

H. I presume that we are talking here about a change of consciousness. What dynamics underlie this change? How can relaxing the body open the mind?

D. In a relaxed state people move from the range of beta brain waves to alpha, from a brain wave frequency of 14 to 22 cycles per second down to 4 to 14 cycles per second. We look for the alpha state when we come home, take off our shoes, turn on soothing music, and put our feet up. In the alpha state we can learn languages, math, and other subjects much faster than in beta. Musicians and athletes often practice at alpha levels ("skull practice" they call it) before they work on gross levels. Gary Player, for example, does it before tennis matches. I understand that the Chicago White Sox do. I don't think your clients would call them "kooky."

H. So at alpha level, there is more space?

D. Yes.

H. I don't think I understand the significance of space.

D. Space has great mystical significance, but let's look at a very worldly example. In an area where I once lived, a large organization took over a local bank and changed its name and logo. The front page of the flier for the new bank was black. Nothing was on it except four little words printed in white in the lower right hand corner: "X bank is dead." If the commercial artist had put one or two hundred words on the front of the flier explaining what happened and why, the "feeling" impact of the message would not have come across.

Advertising space, physical, mental, and spiritual space—all are vital for success, harmony, and health. Mental space is most vital for peace work. Unless there is space in our minds, we have a hard time hearing what others say. Like an electrical wire in which impedances block the force from coming through it, a cluttered mind does not let the message in. Somebody once said to Thomas Edison, "My! You are a genius! Where do you get your ideas?" Edison answered that he was not a genius. "My ideas come from all around me. They're in the air. When I quiet my mind I can hear them."

H. Would you say that our inner space is more real than the thoughts that come and go on it?

D. Much more real! It is on that screen that the drama of conflict is played. When you watch an emotional movie, it seems very real. You cry and you laugh, and then it ends. The figures that made you laugh and cry vanish. They were figments of imagination. Light clicks off the screen and people walk out. Only one thing is left and only one thing is real—the screen.

Reality:
The Top of the Pyramid
Has Only One Point

Vera called herself a Christian, but her family didn't because Vera never went to church. Divorced and in her late thirties with two active careers, she said she did not have the time to think one way and live another. "I want to be a Christian," she said, "but not through a church. In my town, there's a different church on every other corner. Each one says that it has the right answer, the only right way to God. Rivalry makes no sense to me. Why must there be so many conflicting churches? And how can I reconcile my desire to be a Christian with what my heart knows is wrong?"

D. People have established churches on the basis of their differences with others rather than their similarities. Sometimes those differences relate to very minor points. Another reason for so many churches is that human beings interpret scripture through the prism of mind, and minds differ. Our inherent tendencies, experience, environments, and parental and educational influences tend to sculpture our mental prisms in a way that is unique to each of us. Only in states of mystical contemplation, when the mind is transcended, does the truth of unity become apparent.

Buddhist, Vedic, Taoist, and Christian mystics tell us the same thing.

What lies behind this phenomenon is the activity of mind. The mind erects barriers between people. Mind imposes labels on itself and others: "This is good." "That is bad." "Her way is right." "His way is wrong." "I know all the answers." Only when the mind is transcended can these barriers dissolve. Transcending mind means going beyond the sense of separation.

To reconcile your desire to be a Christian with the truth revealed in your heart or, as you put it, to live outwardly as you think inwardly, study and practice the teachings of Christian mystics, for they have experienced the essence of Christianity. Read the works of St. Teresa of Avila, St. John of the Cross, and the Early Fathers of the Desert.

In the East, the truth of unity and the unity of Truth are described like this: A ray of sun admired its shape. Obviously separate from all other rays, it thought, "I exist independently. My form is different from all other rays. I can see more than all the others can see." One day, the ray happened to turn around and move towards its center. Nearing it, the ray got a shock. Why, it was not at all an independent ray! It was and is the sun! Even more surprising was the fact that all the other rays were also nothing but sun.

Climbing the ladder of spirituality is like climbing a pyramid. At the bottom there are many points. At the top there is only one.

Postscript

Chances are that when you bought *Wisdom, Bliss, and Common Sense* you were looking for some insights. Perhaps you were eager to learn how to conquer anger, jealousy, impatience, or fear; how to release negative emotions; how to meditate and bring meditation into your life. Now that you have read about it, will you suddenly become patient? Fearless? Peaceful? Will you meditate regularly and deeply, and bring meditation into your office? No, not yet. A physician at the Kaivalyadhama Yoga Research Institute in India told me why and what you have to do now.

"Every physical, mental and spiritual transformation," he said, "entails five steps: intake, digestion, assimilation, excretion, and resultant satisfaction. We can't jump from the first to the last step; we have to go through all five."

When we eat, our hands take in food. Then our teeth and tongue act as mortar and pestle: they chew, cut, pull, and press to release enzymes in our mouth that trigger digestion. Assimilation, excretion, and satisfaction follow.

Now let's apply this process to transformation. Just as we take in one morsel of food at a time, we generally do better when we work on one goal at a time. Let's presume that your highest priority is mastery of anger. With your eyes, your inner ears, and your mind, you have just taken the first step: you have imbibed the words that show you how. No transformation will occur if you stop there. To digest what you have read, your intellect must reflect on the words, turn them, churn them, and mull them over until their truth pervades you.

When your intellect has absorbed the message and digestion has begun, you are ready for step three: assimilating or internalizing your intake. This process occurs through meditation. As you bring these truths into the silence, your heart takes over, and the work of further assimilation goes underground to unconscious levels. Excretion, the fourth step, occurs naturally. Let's say that your boss wants a letter typed at ten minutes to five. In the past you would have exploded. But something has changed. Suddenly you find that you can cope with anger on the spot. You feel calm, and that inner calm gives birth to the fifth step: the joy of self-mastery and spiritual growth.

The same five steps apply to liberation—to the transition from thinking that you are a limited body subject to birth and death to the knowledge that you are boundless Being and Consciousness. Television, radio, billboards, magazines, newspapers, and stores tell us that certain perfumes, lotions, drinks, foods, cigarettes, beds, lipstick, and clothes will make us do, feel, and be great things. They will enhance and coddle our bodies, make them soft to touch, sweet to smell, lovely to look at. Enhancing our bodies enhances our worth, they tell us. Millions of times we have been reminded of the great lie—of what we are *not*. To transcend this brainwashed body consciousness, we need to chew, digest, and assimilate the reality of what we *are*.

Once upon a time a lion cub got lost among a flock of sheep. The sheep treated him as one of their own. The cub ate grass, followed them, and bleated like they did. One day a lion passed by. He was amazed to see a cub eating grass. Running after it, he seized it and dragged it to a pond. The cub kicked and bleated louder than ever.

"Stop bleating," shouted the lion. "You're no lamb! Now look in the water."

"Baa. Baa," the cub bleated as he stared into the pond. But when he saw his face, he stopped.

"Why that face is just like yours!" he said. And off they went together.

I hope that, like the pond, the pages of this book will help you shed the illusion of limitation. I hope that more and more you will say to your daily false reminders, "No! I refuse to perpetuate the great illusion! I am not this body. I am the light that perceives the body, the space in which it moves, the love that makes it possible. I am formless and nameless. I am birthless and deathless." I hope you will come to know yourself as infinite Consciousness, all-pervading Light, the Self and the Source of all.

About the Author

Twenty-five years ago, Darshani Deane was initiated into the Vedic tradition in the Himalayas of India, and she has returned to India many times for further studies. Grounded in Vedanta, she also studied Raja Yoga, Tibetan and Vipassana Buddhism, the Gurdjieff Work, and Christian mysticism, under masters in India, Nepal, Burma, the United Kingdom, Africa, and the United States. Over the years, Darshani has meditated in the solitude of forest hermitages of both the East and West.

Born and educated in New York, the author worked her way alone through seventy-two countries as a professional composer, accordionist, lecturer, and writer. She raised funds and taught English for an African school; authored an African *Who's Who*; was an amateur pilot; and the first woman to drive a Land Rover alone from England to India.

For the last ten years Darshani has given workshops on the dynamics of personal and spiritual growth, for the public, industry, churches, and schools. Questions and answers that emerged in these workshops form the basis of *Wisdom, Bliss, and Common Sense*.